IN MISCHIEF'S WAKE

H. W. TILMAN

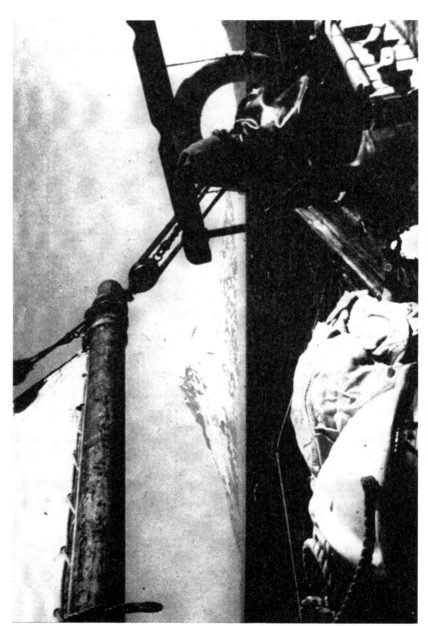

Mischief off Jan Mayen, Beerenberg in the background

IN MISCHIEF'S WAKE

H. W. TILMAN

TILMAN

First published 1971 by Hollis & Carter Ltd
This edition published 2016 by Tilman Books
www.tilmanbooks.com
a joint venture by
Lodestar Books www.lodestarbooks.com
and Vertebrate Publishing www.v-publishing.co.uk

Cover design by Jane Beagley
Vertebrate Graphics Ltd. www.v-graphics.co.uk

Lodestar Books has asserted their right
to be identified as the Editor of this Work

Series editor Dick Wynne
Series researcher Bob Comlay

The publisher has made reasonable effort to locate
the holders of copyright in the illustrations in this book,
and will be pleased to hear from them regarding
correct attribution in future editions

A CIP catalogue record for this book
is available from the British Library

ISBN 978-1-909461-36-9

Typeset in Baskerville from Storm Type Foundry
Printed and bound by Pulsio, Bulgaria
All papers used by Tilman Books are sourced responsibly

Contents

Photographs

Maps

Mischief

Bristol Channel Pilot Cutter built at Cardiff 1906 by Thos. Baker, East Canal Wharf. Length 45 feet. Beam 13 feet. Draught 7 feet 6 inches. Net tons 13.78. T.M. 29 tons.

1906–1919	Working pilot boat owned by William Morgan or 'Billy the Mischief'	
1920	Sold for £450 to a Mr Unna who sailed her to Takoradi	
1927	First appears in the Yacht Register and had subsequently in twenty-seven years ten different owners	
1954	Bought at Malta by Ernle Bradford who sailed her to Palma, Mallorca and sold her to her last owner, H. W. Tilman	
1954	Palma—Gibraltar—Oporto—Lymington	2000 m.
1955–56	Las Palmas—Monte Video—Magellan Straits—Valparaiso—Callao-Panama—Bermuda—Lymington (*Mischief in Patagonia*, 1957)	20,000 m.
1957–58	Las Palmas—Bahia Blanca—C. Town—Durban—Beira—Comoro Is.—Aldabra—Aden—Port Said—Malta—Gibraltar—Lymington (*Mischief Goes South*, 1968)	21,000 m.
1959–60	Las Palmas—C. Town—lies Crozet—Kerguelen—C. Town—St Helena—Lymington (*Mischief Among The Penguins*, 1961)	20,000 m.
1961	West Greenland. Godthaab—Umanak Fjord—Godthaab—Lymington (*Mischief in Greenland*, 1964)	7500 m.
1962	West Greenland. Godthaab—Evighedsfjord—Holsteinborg—Exeter Sound (Baffin Is.)—Lymington (*Mischief in Greenland*, 1964)	6500 m.
1963	Baffin Bay. Godthaab—Godhaven—Upernivik—Lancaster Sound—Bylot Is.—Pond Inlet—Godthaab—Lymington (*Mostly Mischief*, 1966)	6500 m.

Surveyed Dec. 1963 and reported no longer fit for long voyages.

1964	East Greenland: Faroe Is.—Reykjavik—Angmagssalik—Lymington (*Mostly Mischief*, 1966)	3700 m.
1965	East Greenland: Reykjavik—Angmagssalik—Skjoldungen—Lymington (*Mostly Mischief*, 1966)	4000 m.
1966–67	Las Palmas—Montevideo—Punta Arenas—South Shetland Is.—South Georgia—Montevideo—Azores—Lymington (*Mischief Goes South*, 1968)	20,400 m.
1968	Faroe Islands—Akureyri (Iceland)—Jan Mayen. Abandoned in a sinking condition while under tow thirty miles east of Jan Mayen (*In Mischief's Wake*, 1971)	2000 m.

Two mountains and a cape have officially been named after her—Mont du Mischief, by the French, on Île de la Possession, Îles Crozet; Cap Mischief, also by the French, on Île de Kerguelen; Mount Mischief, by the Canadian Survey, Exeter Sound, Baffin Is. near to Mt. Raleigh.

The author gratefully acknowledges permission to quote from the following publications: From *The American Pilot Chart* by courtesy of the U.S. Naval Oceanographic Office; from Professor Gwyn Jones' *The Norse Atlantic Saga* and *The History of the Vikings* by courtesy of Oxford University Press; from *The Arctic Pilot* by courtesy of Her Majesty's Stationery Office; from an article by H. H. Lamb in the *Geographical Journal* by courtesy of the author and the Royal Geographical Society; and from an article in the *Polar Record* by courtesy of the Scott Polar Institute.

Foreword

Bob Shepton

BILL TILMAN HAS BEEN THE MENTOR, example and inspiration for all of my Arctic expeditions in recent years, each of them following in Tilman's wake and having his name attached to their title.

At the end of our 2014 voyage, a sailing and climbing expedition to Greenland and Baffin Island, we had left the boat in Sisimiut over the winter. The proposed expedition for the following summer simply had the title 'Tilman 2015 – Sail and Climb', the aim being to sail south down the west coast of Greenland and to climb new routes in Tilman's old stamping grounds of Evighedsfjord, Hamborgerland and Cape Farewell before returning across the Atlantic to my home on the west coast of Scotland.

My Tilman style expeditions were born out my experience of leading a circumnavigation with school leavers from the Kingham Hill School where my role had been Chaplain. Our course for that voyage had included Antarctica, though not with climbing in mind, and the experience had raised in my mind the question of what should we do next?

I recalled how Tilman, in his later years, had bought those Pilot Cutters and sailed off to remote regions in order to climb. I had been a fanatical rock climber myself over the previous twenty-five years, a hobby which I found ideally complemented my role as a school chaplain. Like Tilman, I had also concluded that with a small boat we could reach Greenland and the Arctic, returning within a single summer voyage, a far better use of time than spending the six months at sea required to reach Antarctica.

Our whole experience aboard has been heightened by reading his books with their superb, dry, politically incorrect wit. I remember one of my world class Belgian climbers, of Irish and Spanish extraction, laughing heartily and reading extracts aloud as we sailed between climbs and during the Atlantic passages.

It may be that his books appeal to a wider audience in these cosseted days. Having been brought up during the War and its aftermath I can fully empathise with and admire his austere, tough, minimalist, straightforward, no nonsense and comfortless attitudes to life. I would, however, stop short of giving a terrific rocket to some poor lad wearing gloves when helming across the Atlantic!

During his crossing of Bylot Island, to the north of Baffin Island, he and Bruce Reid carried a tent of the day with climbing gear and food, including sixteen tins of pemmican, 'double carrying' the load because of the soft snow conditions on the glaciers for most of the fifty-three miles from north to south. How they did this, I do not know: he must have been a tough old bird. Two of us repeated their traverse in 2001, but on skis, with a reasonable tent and lightweight expedition food, with the glaciers in 'dry' condition, and we still took ten days to do it. We did, however, manage to take in eight virgin peaks on the way, an achievement which they had been unable to do given the conditions at the time.

Then there was the famous occasion when he put his usual advert in *The Times* for crew, but forgot to mention that he didn't take women. He had to write personal letters explaining to each of the sixteen ladies who applied, giving his reasons! Personally I do not think that his preference for all male crews and the fact that he never married implies that he was a misogynist. We should remember that he was brought up in the single sex public school system of the day and had served in active capacities in both World Wars with distinction, where the fighting was all done by men. Actually I think he rather liked the ladies and by all accounts was always gracious in their company, but in a public school way he was probably a little fearful of them too. Also perhaps he was apprehensive that in the small confines of a boat close relationships might form and become an awkward distraction. I have often taken girls of varying ages as crew with great success and some are still amongst my best friends years later; one year, three of them termed themselves 'Bob's Angels' which I took as a terrific compliment. But on one Arctic expedition out of a number, I have known something of what I suspect Tilman was probably concerned about.

The fact that he was very definitely 'old school' is part of the appeal of the man. You will be aware of the story, I always imagine it was on top of the Ruwenzori in East Africa, when after years of climbing together Shipton turned to Tilman and said 'I think we know each other well enough by now to call each other by our Christian names'. To which Tilman gave a simple reply, 'No'. Or so the story goes.

So, like all of us, a man of contrasts. Tough, unrelenting, almost immovable in pursuing his aims, come what may. Spartan, taciturn, achieving so much, unassumingly innovative. Did he ever brief his crews or tell them what he expected of them, or even where they were going?

I have a tremendous admiration for the man and his achievements in somewhat cranky old boats. While I have followed his example in the Arctic for many years, I have to confess that secretly I am rather glad that I never sailed with him. But then I am also glad that one who did has put me right on that point, thoroughly enjoyed the experience and looks back on his voyages with Tilman with gratitude saying that he'd 'never been happier in my life'. There can't be a greater recommendation than that.

Bob Shepton
March 2015

Preface

THE STORY OF THE LOSS of *Mischief* is recorded here for the first time. There are also accounts of two voyages in her successor *Sea Breeze*, a Bristol Channel pilot cutter like *Mischief* but even older. The most lenient judge would mark the first of those voyages as a failure, but the second, in my own opinion, was entirely successful. We did what we had set out to do and in the doing of it enjoyed ourselves. 'In the joy of the actors lies the sense of any action. That is the explanation, that the excuse.' These words of Stevenson are for me the only answer needed to a question that is for ever being asked—why men climb, or why men sail.

H.W.T.
Barmouth
January 1971

PART ONE

---◆---

Mischief's Last Voyage

Summer 1968

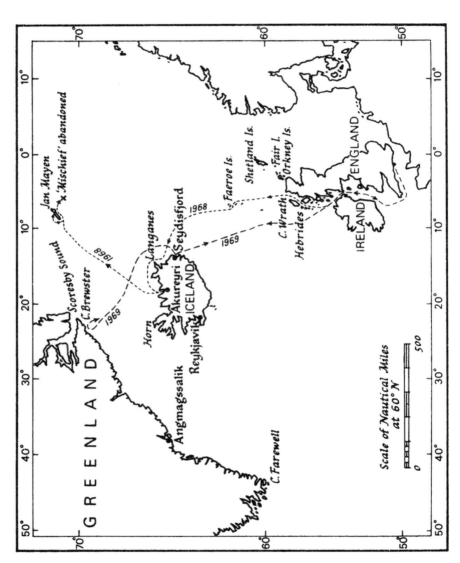

Map 1: To Jan Mayen and East Greenland

CHAPTER I

AN AMBITIOUS PLAN

—◆—

IN THE YEARS BETWEEN 1954 when I bought her, and 1968 when I lost her, the possession of an old pilot cutter called *Mischief* enabled me to visit some remote regions north and south. In those fifteen years she sailed some 110,000 miles. She was not that big, 45 feet long over all, but she was an able sea-boat, kind on her gear and kind on her crew—that is, she did not throw them about. The loss of a man overboard on one unlucky voyage had nothing to do with the boat. All those visits were in search of mountains, and since mountains are the better for being glaciated, the regions visited were either in the Arctic or in moderately high southern latitudes. There is no need to go far south in the southern hemisphere to find glaciers at sea-level. South Georgia, for instance, where the Nordenskjöld Glacier is lapped by the sea, is in the latitude corresponding to that of Whitehaven in Cumberland. In 1966–67 *Mischief* was at the South Shetlands in Lat. 63° S. and in the following year she sank off Jan Mayen in Lat. 71° N. Thus she ranged widely and, had I not lost her, her range by now might have been still wider.

That 1966–67 voyage (described in *Mischief Goes South*) had been far from happy. The loss overboard early on of the one man upon whom I relied, desertions, bickering, more desertions, were a few of our troubles, besides those imposed by the weather in those latitudes. I might have called it a troublesome voyage had I not just been reading about what Hakluyt called 'The troublesome voyage of the right worshipful Sir John Hawkins', a voyage on which four out of six ships were lost together with several hundred men. Even allowing for the fact that in those days most voyages outside home waters were attended by manifold dangers, hardships, and sickness, this appears to a present-day reader as a gross understatement. Trouble is evidently an elastic term and fortunately seafarers of today do not meet with anything that Hakluyt would have recognised as such. As Brer Tarrypin said to Brer

Fox: 'Lor, Brer Fox, you don't know what trouble is. I'm de man what kin show you trouble.'

Nevertheless the constant unease, if no worse, experienced on that twelve-months' voyage came as something of a sickener; enough almost to make one foreswear long voyages and to take to week-end sailing. But owing to her size and the problem of finding crews, a boat like *Mischief* is really only suitable for long voyages, and I had no intention of exchanging her for a handier, modern yacht whose fittings alone would cost more than *Mischief* would fetch if sold. We had been together too long even to think of it. I could not have endured seeing her in other hands, however well those hands looked after her. Not that week-end sailing, the most that the great majority of yachtsmen can find time for, is to be slighted. It is better than no sailing at all and has the great merit that for so short a time much can be overlooked and much can be endured. What does misery matter if we are all miserable together, is all very well, but the period should be short.

Shortness, then, being desirable, the decision to confine future voyages to northern waters had to be taken. It was taken grudgingly. I should have liked at least one more Antarctic voyage, aimed again at Smith Island, the island where, on that last voyage, we had hoped to land and had instead merely looked at. But it would have been time wasted unless by some happy chance a crew of like minds with hearts that beat as one could have been got together; men, possibly, with an expedition background who would not lightly give up what they had undertaken to do. The Southern Ocean and points beyond have a strong fascination—empty seas, lonely, remote, uninhabited islands, and the romance of the sealers and whalers who sailed those unknown seas long before polar expeditions were thought of, sailing admittedly for gain but not ignobly since they staked their ships and their lives.

In penetrating to Arctic shores there may be less sense of achievement, yet there are strange and little visited coasts to be seen and mountains to be climbed. Even the ice-bound east coast of Greenland, or at least the mountains behind that coast, are now becoming well known to the climbing parties that go there every summer in increasing numbers. Since their time is limited they naturally fly there, thus avoiding the delays, difficulties, and dangers—in short, the fun—of reaching the coast by sea. For there is no doubt that this coast is not

the most successful whaling captains sailing out of Whitby, he was an explorer and a Fellow of the Royal Society. Having made his first voyage with his father at the age of eleven, after twenty-five years at sea he went to Cambridge, took a degree, and entered the Church. He was with his father in the whaling ship *Resolution* in 1806 when she reached Lat. 81° 30′ N., then the furthest north yet attained. Sailor, explorer, scientist, scholar, parson—this kind of man is not found nowadays.

By leaving at the end of June and going direct one should arrive off the Sound at about the right time early in August. It would be a pity, however, to lose the whole of June, a pleasant month to be at sea, when the crew might enjoy some real yachting weather, the sort of weather that would do little to inure them to the rigours ahead but would at least afford some compensation. Moreover, with time in hand, we could call at the Faeroes, Iceland, and Jan Mayen. This island is in Lat. 71° N. and only 300 miles east of Scoresby Sound, thus making a convenient kicking-off place; and from the Norwegian weather station on the island we might learn something of the ice conditions off the Greenland coast. More than that, there is a big mountain on Jan Mayen—Beerenberg (7677 feet high). It is an old volcano and therefore not very interesting from a climbing point of view. On the other hand, though lacking in steepness and technical problems, it is all ice from sea to summit and the weather at that height could well be atrocious.

As plans go, this promised to be one of my better ones, a voyage full of interest aimed at two major targets, so that if one were missed we could always say we had been aiming at the other. The boat was ready, there remained only the trifling matter of finding a willing crew. 'Live in hope, if you die in despair,' is the Australian opal-gouger's motto, a motto, that I, too, have adopted after some recent disappointments over crews. *Mischief*, a Bristol Channel pilot cutter built at Cardiff in 1906, seemed to be feeling her years less than her owner. Indeed, provided the man or men who then had her looked after her as well as I had done, I expected her to be still happily sailing the seas while I was twanging my harp. After her last 20,000-mile voyage to the Antarctic she had needed little in the way of repair, but the two mainsails we carried had both seen long service and were worn out. I had been obliged to order a new one and even in 1968, before prices had really begun to get out of hand, this cost an appalling sum, something over

£300. When I grumbled about this to the sailmakers they asked me how many miles I had had out of the old sails. It worked out at about 1d a mile, and with the cost of jib, staysail, and genoa thrown in, still came to less than 2d. Wind costs nothing, so the sailmakers, proud of the lasting quality of their work, thought I was getting my transport cheap. I might have reminded them that over the years, to keep them going, the sails had had a lot of amateur stitching and patching.

Charles Marriott, who had made three voyages in *Mischief*, now decided to make a fourth. He would not wish to be introduced to readers again since he has figured so often before in these annals. Enough to say that he was a retired Army officer, younger than I, who lived alone in a cottage in Cornwall adjacent to the sea cliffs where they climb, being himself primarily interested in climbing but equally at home on the sea. It would be a kindness, I thought, to ask him, and his coming could do me great service. Twice before he had successfully taken on the irksome job of cook. He would not claim to be a chef, no modern Soyer, inventor of stoves and sauces, the self-styled gastronomic regenerator of the Reform Club, but Charles had a cast-iron stomach, a prime necessity for sea-cooks, especially in *Mischief*'s galley which is forward of the mast where the motion is most felt. But to my regret, he elected for this voyage to work on deck, having had enough cooking, and I had to agree. He was not really fit and his eyesight, which had been exceptionally good, had suffered as a result of some obscure incident in a Spanish port on one of those several voyages in boats other than *Mischief* that Charles had embarked on and failed to complete.

Simon Beckett and Kenneth Winterschladen (a Yorkshire-man, by the way) both aged twenty-four and likeable young men, hunted in couples. They had blown into Bodowen one winter evening on the way home from some rough-shoot in Wales. They had heard of *Mischief* at the Agricultural College, Cirencester, where they had met young Stephen Pitt who had sailed with me on the Bylot Island, Baffin Bay voyage. Kenneth professed to cook and volunteered his services as such. 'When they bring you a heifer be ready with the rope,' as Sancho Panza advised. Men with no sea experience whatsoever will volunteer as deckhands, feeling no doubt that they can learn as they go along, whereas in the galley that process would be neither possible nor acceptable. Simon knew a bit about sailing and I was glad to take them both and so complete the crew. The fourth man, whom I had already secured, was experienced in sailing and worked in a shipyard as a shipwright. I regarded him as my key member and within three weeks of sailing, provisionally fixed for the end of May, he cried off, having been offered a better job in another yard.

A friend came to the rescue by putting me in touch with Ian Duckworth, a young man who had served in the Marines and was then waiting to go to a university. He had achieved some eminence as a rugby player and was also a rock-climber so that he promised to be a welcome addition. Thus the crew, collected in this haphazard way, was complete. Except for Charles, whom I had asked in the mistaken belief that he would be content in the galley, choice hardly came into it. The only times I have had to exercise my fallible judgement were when I had advertised for crew, and provided enough offer themselves of their own accord one is reluctant to resort to advertising. I may be wrong but I like to think that many more would come forward if they knew what was afoot. Of dedicated amateur sailors such as members of yacht clubs, I have had hardly any, presumably because they either have their own boat or a friend with whom they usually crew. On the other hand at various times I have had three professionals, officers from the Merchant Navy sailing for a change in an amateur capacity, who sought a closer knowledge of the sea and its moods than can be got from the bridge of a liner or a great tanker. They enjoyed, too, the contrast of proceeding at a leisurely five knots instead of twenty knots with no time schedules to be kept or tides to be caught.

Expecting to sail on May 31st, the crew assembled ten days beforehand. The crew, that is, less Charles who ran true to form by not showing up until two hours before sailing. While busy fitting-out, young Simon managed to strike a jarring note by asking whether I intended carrying a life-raft. The argument that since *Mischief* had been sailing for fourteen years without a life-raft there was no call to carry one on her next voyage, would probably not be accepted as sound. That rigid opponent of change, the Duke of Cambridge, held that there is a time for all things, even for change, and that time comes when change can no longer be resisted. As the Duke himself would have done, I told Simon that I did not propose investing in a life-raft. Besides the cost, somewhere about £120 then, the carrying of one seemed to betray a lack of confidence in *Mischief* or in me, and too much readiness to quit the ship if she got into difficulties. The decision cast a damp over the crew, but not for long. Simon had a brother in the marine store business through whom he could get a life-raft on loan. Would I mind? This removed one objection. I had not suggested it but thought that if the crew felt strongly about it they could attain peace of mind by subscribing among themselves. The life-raft duly arrived and a home was found for it by the cockpit. Strangely enough, at the sight of this white blister installed on *Mischief*'s deck my mind filled with foreboding.

A delay of an hour or so prevented us from getting away on the top of the tide. Since Lymington is blessed by having two high waters this did not matter and the ebb would still be running to carry us through the Needles Channel. We had shipped a new anthracite-burning cabin-heater and had to wait for its chimney to be fitted. We might as well have gone without, the stove never burnt properly and in Iceland anthracite proved to be unobtainable. Hoping to make things easy for the raw crew I put the jib in stops before hoisting, that is to say the sail is rolled up lengthwise along the luff and the roll secured with light ties, so that when hoisted a pull on the sheet breaks the ties and the sail is set. Evidently we overdid the ties most of which refused to break. The sail was not in its first youth and by pulling ever harder to break it out we tore the sail which had then to be got in and another set. So much for making things easy.

With a contrary wind we beat out through the Needles Channel without hitting any of the numerous buoys, a mishap that I have known to happen with a strong ebb running and a novice at the tiller. Outside the wind died so we went over to Swanage bay to anchor, to avoid being swept back when the flood started to make. While there, we repaired the torn jib. The great thing is to have made a start even if our start had been something less than dashing. The cares of the land fall away, all the worries of fitting-out are over, and for the next four months there will be no bills to pay, no newspapers to read. Though we were not yet a thousand miles from the nearest land where, according to Conrad, the true peace of God begins, we were on the way.

CHAPTER II

TO ICELAND

E XCEPT FOR CHARLES, whom I have never known to be seasick, the sea next day took its toll of the crew. Ken battled on manfully in the galley and was first to recover. With a raw crew one must accept the probability that the boat will be shorthanded for most of the way down Channel, that there will be a lot of shipping around, the land not far enough away, and possibly contrary winds. By keeping the boat under easy sail we managed well enough. I even found time to start taking sights, for after eight months ashore one cannot be too quick about beginning again. The tangles that first resulted made me wonder how on earth we should find the Faeroes, or even Iceland which is quite a large island. In the Channel, by closing the land, the lost navigator can generally learn where he is, though in thick weather it would be a mistake to make too free with the shore.

Bound up or down Channel, we have on occasion taken seven days and once only two days. So we were not doing so badly when on the fourth day we rounded Land's End and set a course for the Tuskar Rock. We had our minor worries. The barrel of the bottle screw on one of the starboard shrouds dropped off and with the usual perversity of inanimate objects found its way overboard. Happily we were on the port tack at the time and we had a spare. The mould that at this early stage attacked our stock of hard-baked bread was more serious. This is thickly sliced bread rebaked that, when so treated, usually lasts for the outward passage. This had not been rebaked enough, consequently we had to start on the 'Lifeboat' biscuits normally held in reserve. Baking at sea for five men on a Primus stove is not really on. There is first the difficulty of finding a warm place where the dough can rise; and then the limited oven space that would permit of only one loaf at a time, a loaf that would vanish at one meal. The cook would be at it all day and every day, and the consumption of paraffin would be frightening. If I may be permitted a toot on my own trumpet, I, who consider myself a master-baker, would not undertake it and would not guarantee the results. In one of the present writer's Himalayan books there is a picture of the 'Master-baker' looking ineffably smug, standing by an ice-axe stuck in the ground on which is balanced one of his masterpieces. Making bread in the Himalaya, or at least on the approach to the Himalaya, where there is a hot enough sun to raise the dough and any amount of fuel, is child's play compared with making it on a Primus stove in a boat. I make the bread at home but as I am the only one who eats it the task is not onerous.

With bread and iron one can get to China, as the French Revolutionary commissars (who had no intention of trying) liked to tell their ill-fed and ill-equipped troops. We were merely going to the Faeroes and had plenty of biscuit. Having passed the Tuskar and later the Arklow lightship we soon had in sight the Isle of Man and Scotland. The expensive new mainsail set beautifully and we now had it down to haul out once more the head and the foot. If this stretching is not done with a new sail the leach goes slack and may remain slack, flapping incessantly, wearing out itself and the patience of the crew. They were by now beginning to know their way about, how things should be done and what should not be done, such as, for example, reading a book or even trying to play chess when on watch. Normally we keep single watches so that the man at the helm is in sole charge of the deck and responsible for the ship's welfare. He has not only to watch his steering but keeps an eye on the gear, the sails, any other ships, the sea, the sky, and anything else of interest. If this is done conscientiously there should be no question of boredom or any need for its relief by reading a book. Nevertheless it is not uncommon nowadays for yachts that are not going to be sailed single-handed to be fitted with self-steering gear so that the crew can avoid the tedium of having to steer. One presumes there is still someone on watch even if he is not steering. I should have thought that those who can only get away to sea for brief periods would be only too happy to steer, to feel a boat under their hands, and be jealous of time so spent.

On the evening of June 9th we were off the Maidens north of Belfast when, as had happened before, the wind died and the tide turned against us. To avoid losing ground we anchored in Glenarn Bay, a few miles south of Red Bay, the anchorage we generally used.

Without waiting to be piped to 'Bathe and Skylark' the hands bathed and rightly complained of the cold. North of Rathlin Island, which we passed next afternoon, there are numerous overfalls marked on the chart as 'dangerous in unsettled weather'. One could well believe it. With the weather extremely settled, the sea glassy and no wind at all, these overfalls were boiling away, showing like white water breaking on a roof. On a lovely, still summer evening, disturbed only by the fog signal from Rathlin Island, we drifted along the south coast of Islay, until at midnight, the tide in our favour and under a full moon, we shot through the Sound of Islay at five knots. This welcome spurt was but brief. Anti-cyclonic weather, haze and light airs, persisted as we slowly worked our way north through the Minches. Had we been able to see anything, the mountains of Skye for choice, it would have been pleasant enough. Too pleasant, really, because the crew were not yet fully seasoned, as they realised when at last we had cleared the Butt of Lewis and met some wind and sea. All were unwell again except, of course, Charles. Sula Sgeir is a rocky, uninhabited island about thirty-five miles north of the Butt of Lewis. We passed close by it at mid-day of the 15th, going fast under reefed main and small jib. That night, with supper reduced to soup and cold bully, one realised that speed and comfort are seldom compatible.

Approaching the Faeroes from the south on an earlier voyage we had run into trouble when we found ourselves in a fierce adverse current and a confused sea some five miles south of Syderø, the southernmost island. On that occasion we had been nominally making for Thorshavn on the east side of the Faeroes but our plans were sufficiently elastic to allow us to turn sail and make for another harbour on the west side. There are altogether eighteen islands spread over some sixty miles of sea. Harbours abound, most of them 'summer harbours' and a few classed as 'winter harbours' reputedly safe in all weather conditions. On this voyage we had some obligation to make Thorshavn, the capital, as I had promised to meet my Danish correspondent Captain Toft who would be there in his survey vessel *Ole Roemer*. Thorshavn is on the east side of Strømø, the largest and most important island. Owing to cloudy weather we had had no sights for latitude and only a snap sight or two for longitude so we steered to keep well to the east of the islands. When on the morning of the 17th we began closing the land the wind faded away and we soon found ourselves being swept by a swift-running current into the well-named Dimon Fjord between Syderø and Sandø. We identified our position by luckily sighting the two unmistakable islands of Lille Dimon and Store Dimon which one would naturally, and probably wrongly, translate as Small Imp and Big Imp. The Small Imp looks like a haystack and they are both over 1200 feet high. Such heights are not remarkable in the Faeroes where, especially on the northern and western islands, there are even greater cliffs, the home of innumerable sea-birds. By running the engine flat out we at last got clear of Dimon Fjord and we kept the engine going in order to catch the north-going tide that would take us into Nolsø Fjord, the approach to Thorshavn. Fog then came down in earnest, reducing visibility to less than 500 yards. All was not lost for we soon heard the foghorn from the lighthouse at the south end of Nolsø Fjord, at first ahead, then abeam, and finally drawing aft. A wraith-like steamer passed us, we caught a momentary glimpse of a mysterious ketch towing a dinghy, and then we almost ran down a lone man in a dory shooting guillemot. It is no disgrace to ask, at least not in thick fog, so we hailed him and were told to stand on until we heard the nautophone on Thorshavn pierhead.

Having passed the pierhead, vaguely visible in the fog, we made a tour of the small harbour looking for some resting place other than the wharves used by fishing and commercial vessels. At length we made fast to an untenanted buoy, having first to launch the dinghy, the buoy having no ring. All formalities were waived by both harbour-master and Customs from whom I learnt that *Ole Roemer* was out but would be back in two days. We had a bath and supper at the Sailors' Home—no bar, no beer. Moored close to *Mischief* was a beautiful ketch named *Westward Ho*, built at Hull in 1880, and now maintained in tip-top order by the community as a show-piece. She has no engine and had recently sailed to Copenhagen. The Faeroes, by the way, belong to Denmark but have their own flag and a modified form of home rule. The flag is easily confused with the Icelandic flag and I once committed a *faux-pas* by entering Reykjavik flying the wrong courtesy flag. I gathered that *Westward Ho* made the Denmark voyage every summer to show her off and possibly to raise funds for her upkeep. Like most, though not necessarily all islanders, the Faeroese have the sea in their blood. Fishing is their main standby. In the harbours of West Greenland one meets Faeroe-Island boats of about the size that we would deem suitable for inshore fishing. The crew of three, augmented when hand-lining on the Greenland banks by two Greenlanders, bunk in a fo'c'sle the size of *Mischief*'s peak where the sails are stowed, and their galley resembles a small wardrobe lashed on deck amidships. If you want to see what's cooking you open the wardrobe door and go down on your hands and knees, for the little gas-ring is at deck level.

It is a mistake to think that as one goes north, morals, like the climate, become more severe. The day after our arrival we had two bottles of rum and a bottle of gin stolen in broad daylight by some youths who boarded the boat from a dinghy while Charles watched unsuspectingly from the shore. Since the Faeroes are theoretically 'dry' hard liquor ranks as liquid gold. The police professed interest, even though they knew the lads concerned, and left it at that. Too much should not be expected in Thorshavn. When the shutter of a new camera of mine went haywire I found there was as much chance of having it repaired as there would have been in Barmouth. Rather than having the camera rust and grow fungus at sea, I posted it home.

Ole Roemer having arrived, I had a talk with Captain Toft and we agreed to meet again for a longer yarn and perhaps a convivial evening at Vestmanhavn on June 21st. *Ole Roemer*, which I would translate—certainly wrongly this time—as 'Old Roamer', was a small, powerful double-ender built for working through ice, with some 18-inch thickness of hull sheathed with greenheart and steel plating. She is used by the Royal Geodetic Survey of Denmark. After completing some work at the Faeroes she was proceeding to Scoresby Sound.

When Charles slept ashore at some hotel I was both surprised and relieved to see him back. There was always the chance of his adopting his familiar role of tourist. Once in South America he had been away from the boat for a month 'seeing the country', and at Reykjavik he had embarked on a bus tour along with fifty other like-minded or misguided tourists. He has an insatiable thirst for sight-seeing, merely for his own satisfaction, with no view, such as some of us have, of inflicting his more or less hard-won knowledge on innocent readers.

On the 21st, with a near-gale at north and the glass still falling, we should have stayed where we were had I not engaged to meet Captain

Toft at Vestmanhavn. I believed that with a northerly wind we should find a good lee under Strømø once we had turned the corner at its southern end. Not a bit of it. We sped down Nolsø Fjord in thirty minutes with the wind right under our tail but on turning west into Hestø Fjord between Strømø and Hestø Island, met the wind head on. We might have known. No matter what direction the wind outside may be, in a fjord it blows up or down, usually in the opposite direction to which one wants to go. Even in the sheltered waters of the fjord, a strong wind against an equally strong tide raised a nasty sea against which we could make little or no headway. With the engine going we were no better off, for the propeller spent half its time out of the water.

On an earlier occasion, similarly bound for Vestmanhavn, we had been in trouble hereabouts. But then we were westward of all the islands on a black, wet night with a gale blowing; and although we had got as far as Vestmanna Sund leading to Vestmanhavn, the strong tide in the Sund proved too much. We had turned tail and sought refuge in the small harbour of Midvaag—precisely what we were now obliged to do for the second time. What puzzles me about the Faeroes is that although the rise and fall of the tide is slight—at Thorshavn about three feet—yet the tidal currents round the islands and in the fjords are extremely strong.

We reached Midvaag that afternoon and, whether or not they remembered *Mischief*'s earlier visit, the people were as friendly as before. The crew of a fishing boat lying next to us at the jetty gave us fish and the harbour-master, a Mr Thomson, arranged to take Charles and me for a drive—an irresistible offer to Charles and one from which, out of politeness, I could not escape. Motoring on Vaago Island is simplified by the fact that there is only one road and that on it there are no competing cars. There may have been another car on Vaago but it was not out that day. The road winds below treeless grass hills past a big lake, Sorvaags Wand, a remarkable lake in that instead of a river outlet it spills abruptly into the sea over a natural weir nearly 150 feet high. After a brief stop at the infrequently used airfield built, like the road, by British troops during the last war, we went on to Sorvaag, a small fishing harbour at the end of the road. Over coffee there we learnt once again that the chief import to Vaago consisted of sheep's heads from Aberdeen. We had been told this in 1964 and found it hard to believe, seeing that the sheep on the island, all with heads, far out-number the population.

Back at Midvaag, we at once cast off to continue the passage to Vestmanhavn where I hoped we might still find *Ole Roemer*. At the entrance to Vestmanna Sund there is a great, gaunt cliff called Stakken and beside it a detached pinnacle over one thousand feet high look-ing like a gigantic Napes Needle. It is called the Troll's Finger. While intent on tracing an imaginary route up this challenging rock spire we sailed almost close enough to be within that hypothetical biscuit's toss. The fjord favoured us with the customary head wind so that we had to motor most of the way to Vestmanhavn where there was no sign of *Ole Roemer*. We therefore continued through the fjord to the open sea where we found a big swell running and no wind at all. We spent an uneasy night.

As this is the last mention of *Ole Roemer* and Captain Toft, I might insert here part of a letter from him showing how he fared. It confirms the wide extent of the ice that year and shows that even professionals have crew troubles. The 'Storis' he mentions is the Danish name for the East Greenland pack-ice. It means large ice:

> We had a lot of trouble with ice during our trip to Scoresby Sound. We met the Storis already a few hours after we had passed Lan-ganes in Iceland, and we only got out of it just before our arrival at Scoresby Sound. We did not get through the Storis without being damaged. The port rail smashed in and the rudder stock twisted about 5 degrees. That was the material damage. The crew could hardly face it, which made the last part of the voyage a bit difficult. The sailing in Scoresby Sound was easy. Fine weather and sunshine nearly every day. The trip home went well without trouble from ice.

After a night's tossing about, only Charles and I could face breakfast, but soon the swell subsided and a fine northeasterly breeze sped us on our way. A sprinkling of snow at the north end of Strømø, where the hills rise to over 2000 feet, reminded us that we were getting north. The sea temperature remained at 50° F. and the air 46° F. I had picked on Akureyri, a port midway along the north coast of Iceland, as the place at which to refresh before going on to Jan Mayen. This involved

the rounding of the Langanes Peninsula at the north-eastern extremity
of Iceland about which the *Arctic Pilot* has some discouraging remarks:

> The neighbourhood has a deservedly bad reputation on account of
> the frequent fog and strong tidal streams and currents, and the unre-
> liability of the magnetic compass in the vicinity, all of which have
> contributed to the loss of many vessels. Moreover additional dan-
> gers and difficulties may be caused by the presence of polar ice, and
> finally, Langanesröst, a heavy race, may extend far out to sea even in
> calm weather.

Of these manifold perils we might, I thought, safely discount the ice.
At the end of June, though it might still be off Horn at the north-
west corner of Iceland, it would hardly extend so far east as Langanes.
In the light of Captain Toft's letter this optimism was ill-founded; he
gave no dates in his letter but he was probably there a week or so
before we were.

On June 25th we experienced a sudden drop in the sea temperature from 48° F. to 39° F. and on the following day we sighted land
some twenty-five miles to the south-west. Intent as we were on giving
Langanes and its dangers a wide berth, a strong westerly set seemed
equally intent on pushing us into the land. Langanes, when first
sighted, bore north-west but by the afternoon of the same day we were
well inside it with no hope of weathering it on that tack. We were reluctantly steering south-east on the other tack when an Icelandic Fishery
Protection vessel bore down on us. Our consciences were clear, we had
not even a line out over the stern, for I have long abandoned hope of
catching fish near the surface in northern waters. On the next tack we
must have had everything in our favour. We passed close under the
dreaded promontory without let or hindrance, the weather remaining
bright, the compass behaving as usual, and even Langanesröst seemingly asleep. It is a drab looking peninsula running out to the north-
east for some six miles, high and perfectly flat with yellowy-red cliffs
dropping to the sea. There is a lighthouse at the extremity which we
rounded less than a quarter-mile off on June 28th. One of the numerous small boats fishing in the vicinity came near enough for the crew to
thrown nine large cod on to our deck.

Langanes in Lat. 66° 23′ N. is only seven miles short of the Arctic Circle. On rounding it we steered north for more than this magical seven miles in order to clear the next cape. It seemed strange to cross the Arctic Circle under twin staysails, a rig that I always associate with trade winds and tropic seas; but there we were bowling along under the twins on a cold, brilliantly fine day with snow mountains ranging all along our port hand. We were passed first by a cargo vessel and then by three sea-going swans, while high overhead the geese were flying north. That night the sun remained just above the horizon so that even at 1 a.m., we had no difficulty in making out the entrance to Akureyri Fjord.

CHAPTER III

TO JAN MAYEN

A KUREYRI LIES THIRTY MILES INLAND at the head of a fjord properly called Eyjafjordhur. The *Pilot* refers to the fjord as 'the most
populous and most frequented inlet on the north coast, and is one of
the places where the herring fishery is of considerable and increasing
importance.' Written in 1949, this hardly holds good today. Herrings
are no more set in their ways than restless mankind and they have now
almost completely deserted the north and east coasts of Iceland. The
several herring-oil factories dotted along the fjord lie idle.

The fjord is wide and we tacked up it, hoping to astonish the
natives by working in under sail. As we drew near the town that
evening the wind failed and we turned on the engine. How often does
one write those words—always with a slight feeling of guilt, that it
is not quite playing the game; and how comparatively easy does the
action itself make life at sea—no drifting about in fog off Thorshavn at
the mercy of strong currents, wondering which bit of the coast you are
going to hit; no drifting helplessly off Akureyri in the rain wondering
when the bars close.

At Akureyri, apart from the commercial wharf, there is a so-called
main harbour with a narrow entrance that looked small even by our
standards. So we finally anchored in four fathoms off what looked
like the Town Hall to make enquiries. By now rain fell heavily, but
it was a Sunday evening and the rain had by no means stopped the
rush to the coast which, just as in England, was in full swing. The
road ran along the sea-front and the sight of a strange boat from England anchored nearby soon caused a traffic jam as one by one drivers
stopped to look. Rowing ashore and climbing up the sea-wall on to
the road I accosted the slightly astonished driver of the nearest car.
Fittingly enough he happened to be a Customs officer who, in spite
of being off duty, took me to his office, gave us clearance, and recom-
mended our moving into the main harbour. We lay there in perfect

peace, disturbed only by an occasional lorry and the dust it raised from the untarred dock road.

In the evening we entertained the harbour-master who brought us our mail. After lamenting the disappearance of the herring and its consequences for Akureyri, he told us that only a fortnight before the

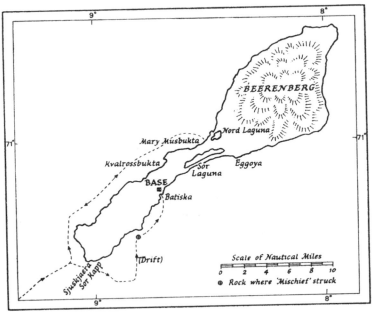

Map 2: Jan Mayen

fjord had been half-filled with ice. We had indeed noticed one or two small floes aground on the shores of the fjord. Despite the wet day, he told us that they were having the finest summer that northern Iceland had enjoyed for many years; in fact the same held good for Norway (as we found later) and the western half of the British Isles. Herring or no herring, Akureyri seemed to be thriving, motor cars thick on the ground and new houses and roads being built. It is in a favoured region for sheep and dairy farming, and the three hotels testified to an increasing tourist industry.

Though the resultant heat had been slight we had already burnt our anthracite and wished to buy more. No one in Akureyri used the stuff but we could have a bag sent up from Reykjavik 150 miles away for £10. Feeling like Stanley Holloway's Yorkshire Noah who declined paying three halfpence a foot for the bird's-eye maple needed to panel the Ark's saloon, saying he would 'rather be drowned than done', I decided to do without. The crew, young and presumably hardy, ought not to mind, while Charles and I, old and frail, would have to buy more sweaters. Meantime Charles, taking advantage of the blazing hot weather that had now returned, almost persuading him to buy dark glasses and a sun helmet, adopted his tourist role and departed by bus for Myvatn Lake. This picturesque lake, dotted with volcanic islands and alive with water-fowl, is a great tourist attraction. I learnt later that he had slept out by the lake, either to commune with the water-fowl or, more likely, since he has a frugal mind, to avoid paying for a bed. Anyhow he returned from Mytvan with a painful arm, diagnosed by a doctor as arthritis, and asked me to delay sailing until he was satisfied he would be all right.

The three youngsters decided to go for an all-night walk to climb a peak about ten miles away. The neighbouring mountains run up to about 5000 feet and still had on them a lot of winter snow. It is not likely to be permanent snow. Less ambitious, I started alone at the more reasonable hour of 8 a.m. for a peak about five miles away. The technical problems were all at the start, finding a way through the surrounding farms without getting into trouble by climbing their wire fences. On the wrong side of the valley there was a good road leading to the Ski Hotel and its ski lifts high up on the opposing slopes. On a hot, flawless day I had the satisfaction of treading the more or less eternal snows, and reaching the top at mid-day, spent an hour there basking in the sun. A fatiguing climb but not altogether unrewarding. It encouraged me to think that with the aid of a halfway camp I might yet reach the top of mighty Beerenberg.

Before I left for my excursion the other three had got back from theirs and naturally retired to bed rather the worse for wear. They were still there when I got back at tea-time, so a little unfeelingly I routed them out and set them to cleaning up below and sorting out a bag of potatoes which was smelling to high heaven. At sea such routine duties are done as a matter of course and it is a bad sign when a crew have to be told to do them. In harbour there is a tendency of some crews to regard the boat as a hotel which they can leave in the morning to go about their affairs and return to at night, trusting that the hotel porter—that is the skipper—will have done whatever needs doing.

The Hull trawler *Portia* came in under tow for engine repairs. Only after she had gone did we learn that the trawler that towed her in had on board a large stock of anthracite. I had a talk with *Portia*'s skipper who invited us to take our meals on board. Reputedly she had the best cook sailing out of Hull, as we could well believe when we had our first meal in the crew's mess. Before the break-down she had been fishing off Horn at the north-west corner of Iceland with a lot of ice in sight. There was evidently more than the normal amount of ice about for the time of year and *Portia*'s skipper did not think much of our chances of reaching Jan Mayen. He felt his own luck was out. They had almost completed their catch just before the engines broke down and the whole had to be sold in Akureyri for what it would fetch as fish-meal. Apparently her engines were something special and the fault in them baffled both her own and the local experts. An electrician familiar with them had to be flown out from England with the necessary part in his pocket or in a suitcase and within an hour of his arrival *Portia* went out for a trial run. On the next day she sailed for the fishing grounds and a fresh start.

Our restaurant having, so to speak, closed, it was time for us to go, and after waiting yet another day on his account, Charles at last agreed to start. We were not really pressed for time and I felt that the delay and the hot weather combined could not fail to improve our chances with the ice. So we sailed on July 7th and this time began tacking *down* the fjord. Rather than spend the night thus occupied, allowing no one any sleep, we stopped at a place called Hjalteyri where we secured to the jetty of a herring-oil factory. It appeared not to have been in use for several years. A crowd of youngsters had watched us come in and without a word the crew went off with them to the nearby village, two arriving back at 3 a.m. and young Simon, our Don Juan, at breakfast time.

We reached the open sea that morning, passing the stern trawler *Pricella* from Fleetwood at the fjord entrance. Twenty miles from the coast is Grimsey, a small, grass-covered, inhabited island which we failed to see, leaving it well to windward. Another island, Kolbeinsey, uninhabited, lies thirty-six miles north-west of Grimsey beyond which there is nothing until one reaches Jan Mayen some 300 miles north of Iceland.

So light was the wind on the following day that we had the genoa set. Some ominous fog banks lay on the horizon ahead and by nightfall we were in the thick of one listening apprehensively to the beat of an approaching engine. We had a glimpse of the vague outline of a small fishing boat before it vanished in the fog, but then the noise, instead of receding, seemed to draw near again. Once more the boat appeared out of the fog and this time came in close while a man shouted across to warn us of ice five miles to the north-east. This was a seamanlike act and we thanked them warmly for the unwelcome news. By ten o'clock we could hear the distant growl of pack-ice and shortly after sighted an outlying floe. Sea and air temperatures were both 35° F. So close to the ice, the fact that the sea temperature was no lower seemed to indicate that this was a detached field of no great extent. Soon we had floes on either hand and hastily handed the genoa to reduce speed, having all our work cut out dodging floes and steering a course that would have made an eel dizzy. As the ice persisted I altered our general course to east and finally south-east. We began to draw clear and soon after midnight had passed the last straggling floe.

By morning we were out of the fog-bank and enjoyed a fine sail all the day, reeling off ten miles every watch. A noon sight put us at 67° 25′ N., 17° 50′ W. I spent the next two days in bed with a bad go of 'flu and since there was practically no wind we could heave to without any sense of time wasted. I hoped that the 'flu had been picked up at Akureyri and had nothing to do with our living in an unheated cabin. Weakening at the last moment I had invested in a bag of coke, cheap enough but more productive of fumes than heat. Usually at sea, since we are not racing, we try to avoid disturbed nights by making no unessential sail changes. On the night that has stuck in my memory on account of disturbance there was barely enough wind to justify our keeping the sails up. Having come off watch at midnight I looked forward to six unbroken hours sleep. The first two hours passed quickly enough as I listened to the sails slamming, until at the change of watch I went up to help set the genoa, hoping that would get her moving. Halfway through his watch at 3 a.m. Charles came down to whisper some tidings, thinking apparently that by whispering he could impart what he had to say without waking me. I never discovered what the good news was, probably some weather secret. An hour later I got up to open the skylight, feeling that we were being poisoned by the stove. At last at 4.30 a.m. I slept and dreamt, dreamt so vividly that I had cut a finger that I woke at 5.30 to stop the bleeding. By then my six hours unbroken sleep were nearly up and it was time to get into oilskins to go on deck for a rest.

In these waters, properly known as the Greenland Sea, cloudy weather and fog are a serious hindrance to navigation, that is unless one had these new-fangled aids such as radio direction-finders. Ideas of what is needed to find one's way at sea have changed. Slocum's ideas about this, set down in 1900, show the extent of the change: 'The want of a chronometer for the voyage was all that now worried me. In our new-fangled notions of navigation it is supposed that a mariner cannot find his way without one; and I had myself drifted into this way of thinking.' As we know, Slocum solved this worry by the purchase of a tin clock for a dollar.

July and August are the cloudiest months and the average number of fog days in summer is ten a month, but ships have been held up sometimes for days or even weeks off Jan Mayen. We were therefore lucky to get a sight on the morning of the 15th and another at noon just before the fog closed down. I reckoned we were then about ten miles to the southeast of South Cape. The chart agents had informed me, wrongly I think, that there is no Admiralty chart of Jan Mayen. The only chart I could find on which it figured in any detail was one where the thirty-mile-long island occupied little more than one inch. The long axis of the island runs from south-west to north-east, the middle of the island being barely two miles wide. Almost the whole of the north-eastern half is filled by Beerenberg's massive bulk. The Arctic Pilot records how in the seventeenth century the island acquired a confusing variety of names:

In the early part of the seventeenth century the island was always being discovered and renamed. Hudson first saw it in 1607 and named it Hudson's Touches. According to Scoresby the whalers of Hull discovered it about 1611 and named it Trinity Island. The Dutch

tradition was that Jan Cornelisz May discovered it in 1611; but this is
a mistake, J. Cz. May of 1611 having been confused with J. Jz. May of
1614, and the name Janmayshoek given to one of the capes, having
been transferred to the island in the form of Jan Mayen. Jean Vrolicq,
the Biscay whaler, claimed to have discovered it in 1612 and named
it Isle de Richelieu. Finally in 1615, Fotherby, the English captain,
discovered it again and named it Sir Thomas Smith's Island. In the
great days of the whale fishery, the Dutch called it Mauritius Island.
In the early part of the seventeenth century the island was in undis-
puted possession of the Dutch, whose occupation extended into the
eighteenth century, when it died out. After a long interval, during
which the island was almost forgotten, Norwegian sovereignty was
proclaimed as from May 8th, 1929.

Normally the island is ice-free from early July until the winter but the
variations are considerable and 1968 was a bad year for ice. Yet on our
near approach to the island and the first sighting of its adjacent rocks
we met no ice at all. We were making for the west coast where, according to my inadequate chart, the Norwegian weather station was to be
found, and were on a course that should have taken us some five miles
south of South Cape. On the evening of the 18th, in fog, at about a
cable's distance, we suddenly sighted and counted seven rocky islets,
the highest about 100 feet high, with white water breaking close off
them to the south-west. These were Sjuskjaera rocks lying about a mile
off Southwest Cape, which is itself about a mile west of our South
Cape. Evidently my sights had not been all that accurate or we had
experienced a strong northerly set. Still it was a great satisfaction to
have seen something, to know that the island was there, and not to be
left in the same doubt as the poet:

> Beyond the clouds, beyond the waves that roar,
> There may indeed, or may not be a shore.

Lord Dufferin describes, or even over-describes in his *Letters from High
Latitudes* a far more dramatic landfall when in 1856 his schooner *Foam*
was off Jan Mayen in mid-July amid quantities of ice. His main reason
for visiting the island was an intense longing to see the great Beerenberg and he tells how the vision was at last vouchsafed him:

Up to this time we had seen nothing of the island, yet I knew we must be within a few miles of it and now, there descended upon us a thicker fog than I should have thought the atmosphere capable of sustaining; it seemed to hang in solid festoons from the masts and spars. To say that you could not see your hand ceased almost to be any longer figurative; even the ice was hid... Thus hour after hour passed and brought no change, while I remained pacing up and down the deck, anxiously questioning each quarter of the grey canopy that enveloped us. At last, about four in the morning, I fancied some change was going to take place; the heavy wreaths of vapour seemed to be imperceptibly separating, and in a few minutes more the solid grey suddenly split asunder, and I beheld through the gap—thousands of feet overhead, as if suspended in the crystal sky—a cone of illuminated snow. You can imagine my delight. It was really that of an anchorite catching a glimpse of the seventh heaven. There at last was the long-sought-for mountain actually tumbling down upon our heads.

Actually, of course, the mountain did not tumble down, and shortly afterwards Lord Dufferin landed on the east coast, leaving a ship's figurehead as a memorial, and departed for Norway. One wonders whether this figurehead has ever been found.

Sheering hastily away from these savage looking rocks we left them at a safe distance before we turned northwards following a coast-line that we had yet to see. Next morning in better visibility we closed the coast and sailed slowly along it about a mile off. We were on the look-out for some landmark that we could identify, Fugleberget for example, described in the *Pilot* as 'an enormous, prominent and per-pendicular rock 551 feet high, the jagged outline of which resembles the broken battlements of a ruined castle... Thousands of birds of many species make a deafening uproar with their cries.' Striking features abounded and we were still arguing about two possible headlands, whether or not they were crowned with broken battlements, when Ken drew our attention to some radio masts which in our search for ruined castles we had overlooked. Turning in we anchored in four fathoms a cable off the beach of a wide bay. This bay, Mary Musbukta, is shel-tered from south and east but wide open to west and north. There are no indentations on Jan Mayen deep enough to afford all round shelter; if caught by a gale from the wrong direction one would have to clear out and endeavour to reach the lee side of the island. South-easterly gales are supposedly more frequent than gales from north-west, so that the west side of the island is the better bet, particularly so since, unlike the east side, it is free from outlying dangers.

There was no sign of life; the extensive hutments clustered near the radio masts seemed deserted. On landing we found them in a poor state of repair, snowdrifts half filling some of the rooms; evidently they had not been occupied for several years. A large dump of coal did not seem to be needed so we collected a bagful to see if it would suit the stove. The *Pilot*'s location of the station did not tally with this; it was said to be half a mile inland at the south end of Nordlaguna, a freshwater lake. We could see the lake but no sign of anything at the southern end. We were 200 or 300 feet above the sea and, looking seawards, could see a line of ice some four miles to the north extending far out to the west. On the beach and on the shore of the lake, which must once have been open to the sea, were masses of driftwood, big logs. These are said to come from Siberia.

Had we but stayed in Mary Musbukta and set about reconnoitring a way up Beerenberg, ignoring the Norwegians, all might have been well. Sooner or later the Norwegians would have discovered us for themselves. Instead, I thought the first thing to do was to make contact with them. Accordingly that afternoon I set out alone to search for the weather station, leaving the others to look after the boat. Charles had retired to bed, as he had been doing off and on since leaving Iceland, so that I could not afford to be long away. Having drawn blank by the lake I crossed a ridge of black gravel and lava in the direction of the east coast. The ridge was the backbone of the island at its narrowest part. On his island Robinson Crusoe was dumbfounded by a footmark. On top of this ridge on Jan Mayen I was equally puzzled by a mechanical digger, sitting forlorn and deserted by the trench that it had dug.

The trench led upwards into the mist but I followed the tracks of the digger downwards and soon came upon a hut; no one was there but it was apparently used judging by four bunks with sleeping bags, skis, and ski sticks. A well-worn track led westwards to the lake. I followed this and found several more huts, all deserted. Back at the first hut I decided to back-track the mechanical digger, to follow the spoor of the monster to its lair, and although the spoor was not fresh one did not need to be a bushman to puzzle it out. Pursuer rather than pursued, I became engrossed in the chase, wondering where it would lead and what I should find.

The tracks led down a steep, sandy escarpment to a vast expanse of beach extending north, south and seawards. A dense but quite shallow fog lay over the beach; from the escarpment I had looked out over it to the sea beyond. The spoor led south but I had now detected a faint distant rumble like the noise of tracked vehicles—tanks, perhaps—out towards the sea. I walked and walked, and still saw nothing. Was it surf making the noise, or possibly ice? No. Presently over the top of the mist I spotted the cab of some vehicle moving south. The whole scene, the sand, the mist, the noise, and a vague reek of exhausts, took me back to the Western Desert. Putting on a spurt—not easy in climbing boots and soft sand—I still looked like being left behind. The truck stopped and then started again coming my way—a Weasel with a crew of six bearded men.

None of them had a word of English so to cut matters short I climbed on board and no one tried to throw me off. Except that I had no beard they must have thought that I had been forgotten and left behind, possibly under a stone, by some Jan Mayen expedition of many years ago. With the tide coming in we began ploughing through the sea until we reached dry land where a jeep and a truck with more men were waiting. I was transferred to the jeep which set off southwards at what seemed a neck-or-nothing race against time, first along the beach, then by a newly-made road, past a landing strip with landing lights on its seaward side, past a large building (the weather station), to arrive at the main base, a huge place, lounge, mess, dormitories, workshops, stores, radio masts, scanners. It dawned on me at last that there was more to Jan Mayen than a weather station. The shadow of the Cold War had fallen upon it.

We were only just in time for the big meal of the day and I could now see why the jeep had almost burst itself. My presence took a lot of explaining to the Commandant as we sat down, fifty strong, to rissoles and assorted trimmings, followed by great slices of cream cake. Not everyone's idea of a balanced diet but after my long walk I had no complaints. The Commandant expressed concern on our account about ice and wanted us to move round to the small bay by the base where they landed their supplies—or maybe he felt he should keep an eye on us. He had already enquired about passports. He told me that a naval vessel expected in had been turned back by ice, so that there was evidently ice about on the east side.

After supper we had a look at the bay, Batiska, which did not seem to me at all inviting, being half-filled with ice-floes. Since we were there uninvited, without even giving notice, I thought it polite and prudent to comply, and undertook to move round in a couple of days by which time the ice might have moved out. It was a fateful decision. Having lent me a very good map of the island, of far more value than our chart, the Commandant drove me by a tarred road back across the island to Kvalrossbukta, a small bay three miles south of where *Mischief* lay. We had missed it on our way up the coast, though the two large oil storage tanks should have easily been spotted. A pipeline follows the road from the tanks to the base. There was also a hut with a radio-telephone of which the Commandant gave me the key; he wanted us to spend the night there as he thought it safer than where we were. At the top of the ridge I left the jeep and walked back to the boat. We parted on good terms. Had all gone well we should have spent a most agreeable time at Jan Mayen, possibly climbing Beerenberg into the bargain. A party from the base had made the ascent and the Commandant promised assistance, advice as to the route and help in carrying our gear to the foot of the mountain.

Dense fog forced us to stay where we were that night; indeed, having made a tentative start we had difficulty in groping our way back. Dense though the fog was, it could hardly have been so thick on the foredeck as to prevent the proper reeving of the anchor chain over its roller when we re-anchored. In the morning we had to break the anchor out by sailing her off and winch the cable in when under way. This had happened once before in a small harbour at Montevideo where there was no room to sail the anchor out. We had had to haul the whole forty-five fathoms of chain out of the locker, drop it overside, and pass the bitter end back through the fair-lead over its roller.

The wind died and we drifted slowly northwards. But for the ice that we had observed to the north we could have gone north about

round the island with the possibility—if fog allowed—of seeing Beerenberg from all sides. In the event we did have a wonderful view when
the next morning dawned cloudless and clear. We were not far away
and the whole mass of the mountain shone dazzling white from sea to
summit. Its great bulk is more impressive than its height, for it meas-
ures some thirty miles round at the base, allowing ample space for
numerous separate glaciers. It is very like a smaller version of Big Ben
on Heard Island which is also a volcano. After being long dormant
it erupted again this year (1970) and the following extract is from a
report obtained from the Scott Polar Research Institute:

> On September 19th–20th the Beerenberg volcano on Jan Mayen
> Island became re-activated after being dormant for several hundred
> years, perhaps thousands of years. Reports by whalers at sea of activ-
> ity on the southern slope of the volcano in 1732 and 1818 have been
> subject to doubt. But steam and carbon dioxide occur in fractures,
> and earthquakes are common.
>
> The present eruption was preceded for one or two days by earth-
> quakes with epicentres which were, however, some distance to the
> north-east. On the morning of September 20th smoke and steam
> rose to 30,000 feet from the north-east flank of the volcano, appar-
> ently coming from a 5–6 km. long fracture with five main parasitic
> crater centres. Geologists from the Norsk Polar Institutt were rushed
> to the island and are observing the activity from land, sea, and air.
> After two days, explosive activity decreased, but a great amount of
> basaltic lava continues to emerge and cascade down the slope to
> build up a new coastal platform at least 500 metres wide and 3–5 km.
> long. Because most of the volcano is covered by glaciers, a great deal
> of melt water has caused floods that have formed deltas.

The upheaval and melting of glaciers must have been a tremendous
sight. On a voyage to Iceland in *Mischief* we once watched the erup-
tion and formation of a volcanic island where the successive explosions under the sea and the uprush of steam, smoke, and ash to a great
height were sufficiently awe-inspiring.

CHAPTER IV

THE LOSS OF MISCHIEF

IN A FLAT CALM WE STARTED MOTORING south until a wind sprang up from dead ahead. As we tacked down the coast the brilliance of the morning faded. Beerenberg's shining splendour was dimmed and finally extinguished and soon we were enveloped in the familiar wet fog. Upon making our final board to the east which I judged would lead well clear of Sjuskjaera, we again sighted those seven rocky fangs close aboard. Unable to weather them we went about and on the next tack cleared the rocks but had the breakers off South Cape too close for comfort. The wind failed and left us drifting, the breakers and some ice-floes close on the port hand. So we handed the sails, motored due east for half an hour, and lay to for the night, the fog still thick.

All this was the immediate prelude to a disaster for which I must take the blame: primarily for not getting far enough away from the coast, a coast off which there were outlying rocks and towards which the northerly set we had already experienced would certainly set us. I had the watch from midnight and in view of the fact that we were not moving or so I supposed, did not spend the whole time on deck but came up at frequent intervals. Ian had the next watch and like a fool I told him that he need not be on deck all the time but to come up frequently. Stupid enough orders! How frequent is frequently? Admittedly it was perishing cold and clammy on deck and one tries to make things as easy as possible for the crew, but there is only one place for the man on watch however safe the conditions may seem. Lying to a mile from a rocky shore in fog, visibility some 200 yards, we were by no means safe. Nevertheless what followed need not have done. Ian must have interpreted my imprecise orders liberally. Had he been on deck any time after three o'clock he must surely have heard or seen something to rouse concern. At 3.30 a.m. I woke to a horrible crash and it hardly needed Ian's hurried dash below to tell me we had hit a rock. On reaching the deck the first thing I saw was a rock pinnacle looming

46

above us—I could almost have touched it with a boathook—and *Mischief* was aground on its plinth bumping heavily in the slight swell. I had lost no time in reaching the deck but the panic-stricken Ian had been even quicker to pull the cord of the life-raft without first launching it; and if that were not enough was even then hastily cutting the dinghy lashings. Had there been any rats on board they could not have been smarter about attempting to leave the ship. The great yellow balloon of the inflated life-raft now obstructed the starboard deck. Over the top of this I imparted to Ian a few first thoughts and told him to stop mucking about with the dinghy. The engine started at once and in a matter of minutes the boat slid off but not before the hull had taken some hard knocks.

She was making a lot of water but not more than the whale pump could handle if used briskly. The only plan seemed to be to beach the boat in the hope of being able to get at the damage. The bay we had been making for was not far off if we could find it, and I felt sure the Norwegians would give us all the help they could. The outlying rock on to which we had drifted, the only rock in the vicinity, lay about half a mile out from the shore; we must have drifted north some three miles at the rate of nearly half a knot. No land could be seen so we steered north-west to close it and the nearer we got the more infested with floes the water became until, when within a cable's length or less from the low rocky shore, we could scarcely find a way through. After some messing about I spotted the runway lights and knew we had overshot the bay. We turned back keeping as close inshore as possible in order not to miss it. In the clear water the rocky bottom showed close under our keel. The bay seemed to have even more ice in it than before, so we anchored off while I rowed ashore to give word of our plight. The Commandant agreed that ice or no ice it would be best to beach the boat there rather than at Kvalrossbukta where we would be too far away for them to give much help.

Threading our way between the floes we ran *Mischief* up on the little beach of black sand at the head of the bay. To my dismay we found that the rise and fall of the tide was a mere three feet, meaning that unless she were hauled much further up we would not be able to get at the keel or even the planks above the keel, where most of the damage must be. Only the forefoot would be clear of the water. The beach shelved steeply, too, so that there would always be two or three feet of water round her stern, the boat drawing 7 feet 6 inches. In order to haul her higher we began the heavy task of lightening her, removing the ballast, emptying the water tanks, and dropping the cable over the side.

We started on the ballast that afternoon and made little impression. Each pig, some weighing 100 lb., had to be hauled up the forehatch, carried across the deck, dumped over the side, and then carried up the beach above tide-mark. Had we left them by the boat they would have soon dug themselves into the sand just as *Mischief* herself proceeded to do. Lying on her side at low water, the floorboards out, she had become untenable. About fifty yards inland and high above the beach was a small wooden hut with four bunks which we now occupied, carrying up bedding, food, Primus stove, and cooking gear.

Work began in earnest next day. The Commandant arranged for one of his men, an engineer and an excellent chap who spoke good English, to give a hand. In the bay they had a big float which they used for landing stores and this was now beached alongside *Mischief*. We rigged a tackle for hauling the ballast up the hatch whence it could be swung across the deck, lowered on to the float and stacked there. Except for a few pigs that could not be reached we soon had about four tons out. Ian, a strong lad, now in an extremely morose mood, nevertheless did the hardest work down below, starting out the pigs and carrying them to the foot of the hatch. Charles was *hors de combat* but the other two worked with a will, Simon and I manning the tackle while Ken stacked them on the float.

On the next day a bulldozer did its best to haul the boat higher and gained but a few feet. I then rigged a stout line to the masthead by which the bulldozer could haul her down, careening fashion. We got her well over but perhaps I was too concerned about breaking the mast to heave down really hard. For I still had every hope of sailing to Iceland where she could have been hauled out on a slipway and made tight enough for the voyage home. Charles, I knew, would stand by the ship, while Ken and Simon, though apprehensive, were game to try. Ian had other ideas. The day we beached her he had arranged with the base for a passage to Norway in *Brandal*, a small sealing vessel chartered to bring stores and due about August 2nd. Had he expressed any regret for what had happened, or sympathy, I might have felt sorry for him. The work on the ballast finished, he sat in the hut, a silent picture of gloom. The only words we exchanged were several days later when I asked him to fetch water and received a convincingly rude reply. Nor did he have much to say to the others, particularly Simon, with whom, as nominal owner of the life-raft, that incident rankled. As there was no CO_2 available for inflating it again the raft was of no use.

Life in the hut, therefore, could hardly have been more depressing. Charles had soon withdrawn to the base where he lay in bed in their sick-room having his meals brought to him. Visitors from the base, to whom we could at least offer a drink, sometimes dropped in in the evening to give us the news or to commiserate. As well as the staff there were four young students out for the summer on an archaeological expedition, searching for traces of the seven Dutchmen who in 1633 were landed to observe through the winter the facilities for whale-fishing. They all died of scurvy, the last survivor, who died just before the return of the fishing fleet the following spring, having kept a diary recording their observations right up to the end. Having no worries other than the possible loss of a boat, it was with some shame that I found on coming to write this account that my brief diary of daily events had stopped the day after we landed.

When the engineer and I examined the port side we found no serious damage, no sprung or started planks, only a lot of spewed-out caulking, Underwater aft, where it could not be got at, a piece of the keel some ten feet in length, and its iron shoe, had broken away. This in itself would not be a source of leaking but a keel bolt might have been moved or the garboard strake started. It was now too late to try to turn her round and haul out stern first, and what with the rudder, the shape of the heel, and the soft sand, it would have been hardly possible. Having covered the suspect parts with a huge tingle of tarred felt and copper we moved the bow round and hove her down on the opposite side. With the starboard side treated the same way I felt sure that the leaks had been reduced though by no means cured. When the tide was in she made far less water.

One of our most frequent visitors, a Mr Holvik, whom I called the Viking, was an enormously strong, red-bearded Norwegian, equally at home driving a giant bulldozer or painting a 200-foot high radio mast.

Mischief beached at Jan Mayen; ice on the way out, the float alongside, line to the masthead for heaving down; the rocks astern were used for slinging the blocks for hauling off

Beached at Jan Mayen; ice in the bay, fog bank in the background

He greatly admired *Mischief*, showing as much concern for her as I did. He propounded a plan to haul her right up out of reach of ice and winter gales on to solid ground near the hut, where in their spare time he could work on her. In the following summer I would return and together we would sail her back to Norway. Much as I admired the Viking—I could well imagine him in a longboat with Erik the Red—I doubted whether even he and his bulldozers could haul *Mischief* that far out. Between beach and hut the ground rose steeply and was the sort of sand that overflows into one's boots. With a cradle for the boat and skids or rollers I suppose it might have been done: the builders of Stonehenge, for example, would have thought nothing of it. One main snag was the attitude of the Commandant who discouraged the idea, rightly so from his point of view, for he foresaw, as I did, that the Viking's plan would inevitably mean borrowing from the base plant, material, and probably time.

Shortly after our arrival ice had moved in and completely filled the bay. Had this happened a day sooner there would have been no chance of beaching *Mischief* there. The ice helped in one way by completely damping down any swell; no waves, hardly a wavelet, broke on the beach. Having done what could be done we began preparations for refloating her. We put back the ballast, all but a ton which I decided to leave out thinking she would be that much easier to refloat. By the time that had been done most of the ice in the bay had gone out except for a line of heavy floes right inshore and probably aground, while outside the bay no ice could be seen. The fact that no waves had been breaking on the beach, owing to the presence of the ice, had lulled us into a false sense of security. Only my engineer friend realised that the boat might now be in peril and urged me to get her off quickly. At the moment though, an unbroken line of floes prevented this. As the result of most of the ice having gone waves now began to break on the beach. Either that night or the next—I had lost count of the days—we had some wind and when I went down to the beach in the morning I found about five feet of the bowsprit broken off lying in the water in a tangle of wire. The float had been shifted from alongside, but not far enough, and even the web of mooring warps we had laid out had not prevented the boat surging about and hitting the float with the bowsprit. We had reefed the bowsprit by hauling it inboard but not completely so.

Sailing to Iceland without a bowsprit would be slow work. Instead I arranged through the Commandant for *Brandal* to give us a tow to Norway. They agreed to this and also to bring out a small, portable motor pump to ensure our controlling the leak while on passage. By July 27th only the line of massive floes fringing the beach still prevented us from getting afloat and ever since the rest of the ice had gone out *Mischief* had been bumping on the sand. As well as doing her no good it distressed me to watch. Floating her off would mean living on board and keeping the pump going until *Brandal* arrived when, perhaps, the motor pump would give us a spell, but the engineer and I both thought we should try. By means of a wire led from the stern to a block slung from some nearby rocks and thence to a bulldozer we tried hauling her stern back into the water. After we had gained a few feet she stuck immovably, that much nearer to the floes through which, anyway, there seemed little hope of forcing a way.

Next day, a Sunday, the Commandant came down armed with dynamite sticks and detonators to see what could be done. A big floe threateningly close to *Mischief*'s rudder succumbed to this treatment, splitting into two after a few sticks of dynamite had exploded alongside. A bigger floe only a yard or so from the port side proved too tough and massive, and I feared that repeated explosions so close to the boat might harm her more than the ice. Having done what he could the Commandant departed.

Towards mid-day the wind blowing into the bay had increased to nearly a gale. The waves rolling in set the floes to rocking up and down and lurching forward, and *Mischief* began to bump even more heavily on the sand. The crew had for some days since lost interest but I rallied them for a last effort to shift her by means of a warp to the anchor winch and the engine. With the wind behind it the water was now deep enough under the stern for the propeller to bite. Their efforts lacked conviction. Ian in particular showing more concern for what would happen when she floated than for the consequences of letting her remain. I thought that with the water so high, a couple of bulldozers might do the trick, and that she might just squeeze through a gap by the big floe. With that in mind I ran to the base as fast as I could and found hardly a soul there, certainly no one with power to act. By the time I got back the big floe that had been close aboard, urged forward by the rising sea, had battered a hole in the hull just below the engine water intake, and started several of the adjacent planks. That evening, in despair, I wrote her off. She was one third full of water, so we took ashore anything of value below, books, charts, instruments.

The Viking came along next morning, refusing to admit that all was lost, more convinced than ever that his plan was the best, and determined to have a go at hauling her out whatever the Commandant might think. Clutching at straws I agreed and persuaded the crew to start taking out the ballast once more. The gale had pushed her higher up the beach and most of the water had drained out. Late that evening the Viking brought down a big bulldozer with which he succeeded in moving her about two yards. The soft sand and the steep ascent, where the real tug-of-war began, were still yards away. Even then at high tide she still lay among the breakers, the wind continued to blow, and the waves rolling in lifted and dropped her heavily on the sand. She was a heartbreaking sight.

The Viking's plan was tacitly abandoned. Either failure had subdued him or the Commandant had put his foot down. Instead, on July 30th, he came down to patch the fresh damage, the Commandant being equally bent on seeing *Mischief* safely away under tow. After a drive round the base stores to collect material, the Viking and I set to work to put on a tingle. But with another gale on August 1st the breakers tore off our rudder. This, I feared, might put paid to towing, but the skipper of *Brandal*, with whom the base was now in touch by radio telephone, reckoned they could still tow. *Brandal* arrived on August 2nd according to schedule, having first fetched up well north of the island in spite of radio beacons, radar, and Loran. The same morning the sea tore off the big patch or tingle. Upon which the Viking and I together sought out the Commandant, hoping that after this last blow he might be persuaded to fall in with the Viking's plan. Obviously for success, the use of men, material, and machines would be required. They were very busy, a lot of work having to be done in what remained of the short summer season, as well as the routine work of the base. The Commandant was therefore right to refuse and to limit his assistance—already

generous—to getting *Mischief* afloat and ready for towing. This proved
to be no easy task.

Accordingly the Viking and I put on another patch. He had built a
stage from which to work slung over the side, and with waves continu-
ally sweeping the stage it proved a wet job. The base had a big whaler
with a powerful engine which they used for ferrying, and that evening
I went out in her to *Brandal* anchored well outside the bay. The skipper
spoke no English and seemed to me a little fuddled; the mate, young
and confident, spoke very good English. At the suggestion of the Commandant they agreed to put on board *Mischief* an electric pump to be
supplied with power by a cable from *Brandal*, to reinforce the little pet-
rol-driven pump that they had brought which was already installed in
our cockpit. I could not see this running more or less continuously for
three or four days, nor were I or any of the crew capable of giving it the
necessary nursing. I had to sign a guarantee against the loss of the electric pump, the implication being that *Mischief* was not expected to last
the journey and that we might have to leave her in a hurry. The tow was
to be on a 'no cure no pay' basis; I urged the mate to take it easy and he
assured me that *Brandal* was no flyer. The Commandant did everything
he could to ensure success and our safety, bespoke for us one of *Brandal*'s life-rafts and arranged for a walkie-talkie set and a field telephone
as well to keep the two ships in touch.

Overnight we rove a 3-inch wire through the big block slung on
the nearby rocks, and passed a 6-inch nylon warp twice round *Mischief*'s hull. At 7 a.m. on August 4th, a fortnight to the day since we
had first put her ashore in this ill-omened bay, the Norwegians rallied in force to get her off. Since we were not going to sail we had
not attempted to restow the ballast—I doubt if the crew would have
consented—but abandoned it on the beach. Light as she was, hauling her off took the united powers of two bulldozers, and the whaler
pulling from seawards. Either she had dug herself in or the sand had
piled her, because at first she refused to budge. So the bigger bulldozer, a real monster in the capable hands of the Viking, dropped its
scoop into the sand and using the sand as a cushion advanced on *Mischief* to push her bodily sideways. Having so to speak broken her out
they then harnessed the two bulldozers in tandem on to the wire, the
whaler took the strain, and *Mischief* slid slowly into deep water. All the

ice that had at first hindered us and that had been her undoing, had been swept away by the gales of the last few days. Simon and I were on board with the petrol pump going. It needed to be for she leaked like a basket.

Having secured to a long warp astern of *Brandal* we remained there tossing about in a moderately rough sea until late that afternoon. We found that we could just keep the water at bay by running the pump for five minutes and resting it for five minutes. Meantime the float made several trips out to *Brandal* and finally took off seven men from the base and the rest of our crew. The young archaeologists and my engineer friend were among those going home. Charles, whom I had not seen for the last few days, was to travel in *Brandal*, while Ken and Ian were to help in *Mischief*. Since we were to be in company, Ian had agreed to come. He had in fact reconsidered his earlier decision when we were still hoping to sail away, but only under certain rigid conditions. As with two unfriendly powers when relations have been severed, his ultimatum was handed to me by a third party. I still have the scrap of paper stating his terms:

1. There must be a transmitter on board.
2. Adequate life-saving gear including another life-raft.
3. A forty-eight hour trial run in the vicinity of Jan Mayen.
4. Direct return to England.

On the whole I thought that the chance of *Mischief*'s survival and the morale of the crew would be better without him on board.

After the float had made its last journey to *Brandal* it came alongside bringing Ken and Ian (who was promptly seasick), the mate and a sailor to make up the towing line, as well as their electric pump, a life-raft, and the walkie-talkie set and telephone. For the tow they used a nylon warp shackled to 10 fathoms of our anchor chain on which they hung three big tyres to act as a spring. The remaining thirty-five fathoms of our chain with the 1-cwt. anchor attached we led to the stern to drop over when the tow started. This served in place of a rudder to keep her from yawing about. The heavy electric cable, to supply current from *Brandal* to the pump, they had merely dropped loose in the sea. Its own weight imposed a heavy strain, no current ever passed, and immediately the tow began they told us it had broken. Had it been hitched to the towing line or to another line, as it could have been, *Mischief* might have survived. It meant that the little petrol pump must function for three days without fail and I did not think it would.

At 8 p.m. that evening the tow started. For the vicinity of Jan Mayen the conditions were good: no fog, no gale, and a moderate sea. An hour later Simon and I, who had been at it all day, went to lie down, leaving Ken and Ian to carry on pumping for the next four hours. With a lot of water sloshing about inside sleep was hardly possible; I brewed some tea and we made do with hard tack. I must have dozed because just before midnight Ken woke me to say the pump had given up; the motor ran but it was not pumping. The crew were ready enough to quit and I confess that the skipper and owner, with so much more at stake, had no longer the will to persevere, a fortnight of toil, trouble, and anxiety having worn me down. Communication with *Brandal* was not easy either with the walkie-talkie or the telephone but she had already got the message. She lay to about a cable away and we were told to bring off only our personal gear. In a final round-up in the dark cabin, already a third full of water, I dropped a note-case and all my remaining money. After scrabbling about vainly in the water for a few minutes I gave up and joined the others on deck where they had already launched the life-raft. Since *Mischief* was not insured this 'trifling sum of misery new added to the foot of the account' hardly counted. The premiums demanded for the sort of voyages *Mischief* undertook were always so high that it had never been worth while to insure her.

Thinking that water might ruin it, before leaving we hoisted the heavy electric pump up through the skylight, having quite a tussle. When the other three had stowed themselves in the life-raft I climbed over *Mischief*'s rail for the last time and joined them. Paddling over to *Brandal* we went on board while three of her crew took the raft back to salvage the two pumps. These met with scant ceremony. The electric pump, that we had so thoughtfully tried to keep dry, was thrown overboard on the end of a line and hauled through the sea to *Brandal*. She was soon under way while I remained on deck in the fading light watching *Mischief*, still floating defiantly, until she was out of sight.

As I have said, ice conditions in 1968 around Jan Mayen were bad. Apart from human failings ice had been the main cause of *Mischief*'s loss or that had certainly prevented her from being saved. For me it was the loss of more than a yacht. I felt like one who had first betrayed and then deserted a stricken friend; a friend with whom for the past fourteen years I had spent more time at sea than on land, and who, when not at sea, had seldom been out of my thoughts. Moreover, I could not but think that by my mistakes and by the failure of one of those who were there to serve her we had broken faith; that the disaster or sequence of disasters need not have happened; and that more might have been done to save her. I shall never forget her.

> The world was all before her, where to choose
> Her place of rest, and Providence her guide.

PART TWO

First Voyage in *Sea Breeze*

Summer 1969

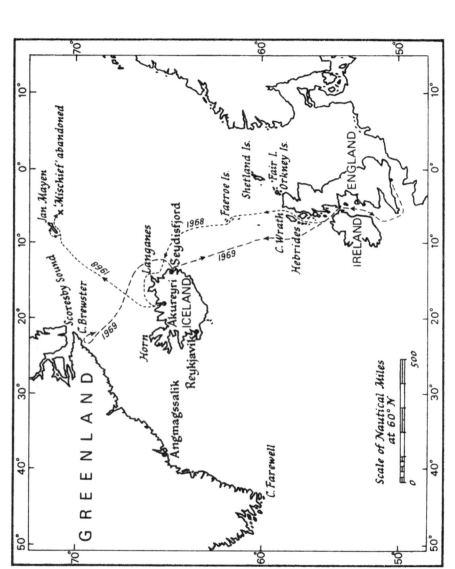

Map 3: To Jan Mayen and East Greenland

CHAPTER V

BUYING A BOAT

O N THE FINE SUNNY DAY that *Brandal* landed us at Bodo in northern Norway it was hard to believe that we were still well inside the Arctic Circle. Without ship or money, but otherwise in fair shape, I qualified as a semi-distressed British sailor. A journalist, who having already interviewed the crew had no ulterior motive, took me in hand and while conducting me round the sights of Bodo persuaded some-one to cash a small sterling cheque. The same day a Norwegian Air Force officer, met casually in the street, did his best to get me a flight to Oslo in an Air Force plane. As there was nothing immediately available he failed to pull this off, but at his instigation I asked for and got from the civil air line a seat at half-price.

At Oslo the British Consul cashed another cheque and introduced me to the people in the Norwegian Ministry of Defence who were con-cerned with Jan Mayen, whom I had made the journey to Oslo to see. I wanted to tell them how much I appreciated the help given us at Jan Mayen and to find out what we owed them. All that copper we had used, for instance, and, far worse, that brand new 6-inch nylon warp that in the attempts to float *Mischief* had suffered such a mangling that it would, I feared, have to be written off. Another item was the food we had eaten and were still eating in *Brandal* which was then on her way down the coast with the rest of my crew. They were inter-ested in the story and assured me that an account would be rendered. When this eventually came it was for quite a small sum on account of *Brandal*.

On the spectacular train journey from Oslo to Bergen I regretted that Charles was not with me to share this great tourist attraction. I quote:

The Bergen Railway is one of the engineering wonders of Europe; it is also one of the greatest scenic railways of the world. All the features

61

which combine to make the scenery of Norway so alluring to visitors
are unfolded along this line in panoramic succession.

How Charles would have enjoyed it. I could see him, for instance, risk-
ing his neck by leaning out of the carriage window when inside the
Gravehalsen tunnel ('3 miles 514 yards and took 12 years to bore') to
take those murky indecipherable photographs in which he special-
ises. He might even have insisted on leaving the train to visit 'the great
Storskvalen glacier to which expeditions can be made.' Nevertheless,
I admit the novelty of looking out upon glaciers from inside an over-
crowded railway carriage, even if the glaciers were a little scruffy and
obviously suffering from an exceptionally hot summer. At Bergen I
boarded the Newcastle boat where, besides finding my late crew, I had
the luck to meet a friend who had been climbing in Norway. Having
his car with him and bound for Wales he thus solved for me the ticklish
problem of reaching Barmouth from Newcastle by rail.

Although something of an addicted pipe-smoker I never find any
difficulty in abstaining if no tobacco is available. In the absence of
a boat there should have been an equal chance of giving up sailing.
The craving, however, was still there and within a few days of returning home I found myself scanning the advertisements in the yachting papers and writing to various agencies. A big boat lying on the
Clyde, magnificent in a photograph, almost tempted me to go north
in spite of some natural apprehension about finding oneself alone and
unsupported in a strange environment, surrounded by men reputedly
dour and undoubtedly businesslike. Were it not even further from Barmouth than the south coast, much could be said for keeping a boat
on the Clyde, thereby cutting out the English Channel and saving at
least a week's sailing when setting out for or returning from northern waters. Having started on the downward path by beginning these
enquiries, the pace naturally quickened. It became not merely a question of finding a boat, taking, too, the ample time that such a search
really demanded, but of finding a boat that was ready or could be got
ready for a voyage the following summer. No doubt, time's winged
chariot hurrying near makes for haste.

The loss of *Mischief* had been fully reported in the Norwegian
press but only one or two English papers had noticed it in a very

brief paragraph. Few people could have known of it. I was therefore surprised when at Lymington, within a month of returning home, I got what seemed to be the answer to my hopes in the form of a telegram: 'Regret loss of *Mischief* can I offer you *Sea Breeze*. Oakeley.' On looking her up in *Lloyds Yacht Register* I found that *Sea Breeze* was a Bristol Channel pilot cutter belonging to Sir Atholl Oakeley. Built at Porthleven in 1899 she was certainly a bit long in the tooth, but no more so, in fact a year less, than her prospective owner. For that was how I already began to see myself; the fact that she was of the same breed as *Mischief* investing her immediately with all the qualities I desired. No wonder Barnum believed that a sucker is born every minute.

More to the purpose, she was lying at Hamble where she could be seen at once and, supposing she changed hands, could be brought to Lymington to be thoroughly overhauled during the winter and raring to go by the time summer arrived. Sucker or not, I did not for a moment suppose that a boat of that age would not need a lot of time and money spending on her before she was fit for a deep-sea voyage. Obviously a boat that is used for day sailing or for short hops across the Channel need not be so entirely seaworthy or so well-found as for an ocean voyage. If only for one's own peace of mind there must be no half-doubts about a boat's fitness for a particular purpose.

There and then I went over to Hamble where I found her lying in a mud berth. The boat was in commission but, the owner not being on board, I could not see below. Superficially she looked in good shape, smartly painted and fully rigged, topmast and all. She had deadeyes and lanyards for setting up the shrouds, eminently more in keeping with a boat of that type and vintage than *Mischief*'s rigging screws. The bobstay, too, the forestay and topmast forestay, were all set up with tackles instead of rigging screws. Certainly in keeping, but carrying things too far, I thought, unless one believes in having plenty of 'give' in the standing rigging. This idea of 'give' had apparently been scotched long ago by Dixon Kemp, an expert writing for Victorian yachtsmen:

> It has been contended that a yacht's main rigging should be stretchable, because, if she were sailing in squalls, if the rigging did not give to some extent, it would be like attempting to drive a railway train by

a succession of blows from a sledgehammer. In stating the case thus ludicrously the fact is entirely overlooked that a vessel's heeling facility affords much greater relief to such shocks than could the yielding property of any rigging, unless indeed the latter were so stretchable as to be perfectly useless as stays. The rigging cannot be set up too rigidly and the less it stretches the better. It was found that in very heavy weather with a ship rolling and pitching heavily, three-fourths of the ultimate strength of the mast and rigging might be tried at any one moment, and that a succession of such trials would inevitably end in disaster.

Compared with *Mischief*'s her cockpit was minute. A mate I had had on one voyage would have heartily approved. He had considered *Mischief*'s cockpit an open invitation to the ocean to come in and fill it, thereby sending the boat to the bottom. Needless to say, on only one occasion had the cockpit been filled to the brim, and then the water readily found its way below whence the pump soon restored it to its rightful place. This diminutive cockpit lay under the shadow almost of a great wooden tiller, the sort of thing John Davis might have had on *Mooneshine*, decorated with spirals running the entire length and culminating in a cunningly carved Turk's Head. I could see myself grasping this massive masterpiece, smiling with content. Striking a more modern note was a large hydraulic winch just forward of the mast that served both as anchor winch and for hoisting the mainsail by means of chain halyards. I believe this had been fitted by a previous owner addicted to single-handed sailing where obviously the main problem in a boat of this size would be that of hoisting the correspondingly large and heavy mainsail.

Other vital statistics for *Sea Breeze* are: overall length 49ft, waterline 43ft, beam 14ft 3in, draft 7ft 5in, sail area 2100 square feet. She was fitted with a Kermath two-cylinder diesel engine. Thus she was three feet longer than *Mischief* and one foot wider, and their respective gross tonnages were thirty-three and twenty-nine tons. When first built, I am told, she was several feet longer. Concerning this I have a letter from one who served in her when she was a working boat in 1911. Mr Tom England writes:

The *Sea Breeze* was built by Bowden of Porthleven to the order of Mr Morgan Griffiths, a Newport pilot. Now Mr Griffiths was never a pilot to go too far to the westward and when he saw the *Sea Breeze* he said that she was too long and too big for him. So he gave the order for her to be shortened but of course her beam could not be altered so he had to accept her shorter in length but with the same beam. He was a person never satisfied and being fairly well off was able to satisfy himself in many ways; so he bought a smaller boat and sold the *Sea Breeze* to Mr Goldsworthy and in 1911 I was transferred to him to finish my apprenticeship. From my first trip in her I was happy. She was light on all her gear and never failed to stay in any kind of weather, even when she carried her forestay away and we worked her for a week with just the mainsail and jib. With the foresheet and jib sheets half drawn and four rolls in the mainsail she would sail herself and make good headway, and she was very comfortable when one was down below. When she was hove-to with the sheets to windward and the helm hard down she made very little leeway. She was not so good as some cutters when beating to windward but when reaching and running before the wind she was great. I would never wish to be in any other craft whilst she was about.

A fine tribute to a fine old boat.

A week or so later I went down again to meet Sir Atholl Oakeley and to be shown over his boat. One could not help comparing her with *Mischief*, the only boat of any size that I have ever owned and accordingly my standard model—the only one I have—for judging what a boat ought to be like. Well, perhaps, not quite. She had some faults. The siting of the galley, for instance, forward of the mast where the motion is most felt, whereas in *Sea Breeze* the galley was well placed between the saloon and the cockpit. In *Mischief*, by having the bunks in two tiers, one on top of another, the whole crew were accommodated in the main cabin or saloon, making for mateyness or unpleasantness as the case might be. *Sea Breeze* had only two bunks in the saloon, two more amidships and forward, while the owner had a cabin to himself with a double bunk, a bunk that, like the proverbial goose, was too big for one and not big enough for two. There were even doors, but these, I reflected, could be easily demolished; for the inside of a boat should be like a church where you can see from one end to the other, the few necessary bulkheads having openings but no doors. The galley had a gas stove and when Lady Oakeley brewed tea for us one realised how painless gas could be compared with the routine of priming and lighting a paraffin stove. On the other hand no one wants to be unexpectedly blown up, and on a long voyage there would be the necessity of carrying a battery of cylinders on deck. True, we had done this without any trouble in *Patanela* on the Heard Island voyage, but she was a bigger boat with high, solid steel bulwarks instead of light wire guard-rails. However, as yet there was no need for me to contemplate throwing the gas stove overboard, for the boat still belonged to Sir Atholl; but since I had not seen anything to put me off completely we discussed terms, the upshot being that I would buy the boat subject to survey. To carry that out the best place would be at Lymington where the Berthon Boatyard had a slip available for hauling her out. Impatient to know the worst or the best, I had imagined that the owner and I would cast off there and then, or at least when the tide served, to motor round to Lymington. I found there were several objections to this, the principal being that the boat would not be afloat until the next spring tide. In the end I had to arrange for the boat to be towed round and met with another snag. For some odd reason the act of towing needed covering by extra insurance. On the face of it a boat under tow with presumably someone steering and an anchor ready to drop would be at no more risk than a boat under its own power.

The tow took place safely, she was slipped on arrival, and a surveyor friend of mine began work on September 25th. I took care to be there. Like *Mischief* and other pilot cutters there was an awful lot of boat below water so that on the slip she looked huge. The men in the yard, who from force of habit kept on alluding to her as *Mischief*, thought I had found a worthy successor. As a surveyor taps and probes his way round a boat there is no call for him, even in the presence of a prospective owner, to conceal his emotions as a doctor must when tapping and probing his patient. On the first day nothing much amiss came to light, but as the survey progressed John Tew's face lengthened until it was as long as the list of defects that he ultimately drew up.

An estimate of what it would cost to have these put right proved to be formidable. Nor would that be the end. Estimates never are the end, especially with a boat, because while the work progresses more faults are inevitably exposed. A survey is bound to be more or less superficial. Short of having the boat pulled to pieces, and in the event of 'no sale' incurring the expense of putting it together again, one cannot expect the surveyor to discover all possible defects. Particularly is this so in old boats like *Sea Breeze* that have had a number of owners altering and re-altering, where there are nooks and crannies that only an agile caterpillar could crawl into, and John Tew was no caterpillar. The massive construction, too, of an old boat may serve to conceal defects, though at the same time it means that a beam or a frame has to be pretty rotten before it becomes dangerously weak. In *Sea Breeze*, for instance, John Tew found a soft spot in the stem that he warned me might prove extensive when gouged out and correspondingly expensive to put right. Altogether he advised strongly against buying the boat.

Once before I had flown in John Tew's face, or at least in the face of his advice. It had cost me a lot and I had not regretted it, for I had thereby given *Mischief* a new lease of life and we had enjoyed many more voyages together despite her having been 'condemned'. On this occasion a repetition of such obstinacy would be going to cost a lot more and I finally decided to take his advice. I had to make up my mind quickly. The boat was now occupying a slipway that the yard wanted to use, it being the end of the season with boats waiting to be hauled out. Either John Tew's bore-holes and other minor havoc must be made good for the boat to be returned to the Hamble, or if the work was to be done, the mast must be taken out and the boat hauled up again under cover. So I telephoned Sir Atholl to tell him that in view of what it would cost to have the boat made really seaworthy I could not buy her. Having expressed surprise that so much needed to be done, and made some observations about both the surveyor and the Berthon Boatyard, he finally suggested a substantial reduction in the purchase price. With some misgivings I agreed and *Sea Breeze* had changed hands.

It would be tedious to list all that had to be done. Apart from refastening the hull throughout, which meant burning her off to the bare

Sea Breeze at Lymington,
fully rigged with topmast

Ice-floes off East Greenland

wood, the major jobs were the removing and replacing of the covering boards, the sheer strake and the extra thick plank below the sheer
strake, as well as thirty-two bulwark stanchions and the frame heads
with them. The ballast had to come out and when out was an astonish-
ing sight, worth anyone's while to come and see. Some of the pieces
were so large, weighing 2 or 3 cwt., and so shaped as to fit the hull, that
it almost looked as if the boat had been built round the ballast. There
would be no taking of that out by the crew. Twice *Mischief*'s ballast
had had to be got out by the crew, once in the Patagonian channels
and again at Jan Mayen. For the kind of ballast that *Sea Breeze* had, a
crew of professional weight-lifters would have hardly sufficed. In the
Berthon yard they got it out easily enough by removing the bottom
planks and dropping it through the hole. One would like to know how
it had first been put in at Porthleven in 1899—possibly before the deck
was laid—and I did not see anyone in Lymington in 1968 capable of
putting it back. It did not go back. It was sold as scrap, to the considerable dismay of the chap who was sent to fetch it. In view of what had
happened twice in *Mischief* and might happen again, we put in lighter
pigs that could be handled.

Just as John Tew had feared, the rot in the stem had gone far. It
proved to be a very difficult job and the cement inside and behind the
lower part of the stem made it no easier. As the soft wood was gouged
out and the hole grew bigger and bigger, a colony of Wharf beetles
were discovered. They are a sort of marine hippy squatter and there was
some apprehension that having been dislodged from *Sea Breeze* they
might take up residence in *Sceptre*, the America's Cup boat, lying in
the same shed. Unless she had some rot in her, which seemed improb-
able, there was nothing to fear as the following authoritative account
of Wharf beetles shows:

> Wharf beetle (*Nacerde melanure*), as its popular name implies, is asso-
> ciated with timber on the water-front, the reason being that such
> timber, unless of a resistant species or pressure-treated with preserva-
> tive, is liable to decay, and forms yet another instance of the close
> relation between beetle damage and rot. The beetle is soft bodied, a
> quarter to half an inch long, with a narrow reddish brown body, the
> tips of the wing-covers darkening to black, the antennae long. The

larva is slender, from ½ in to 1½ in long, dirty white, with a yellow head wider than the body, and having behind it on the dorsal surface of the first segment a protruding hump. There are three pronounced pairs of legs. Infestation is not confined to wooden marine works but is found inland in unpreserved soft wood culverts and like places where the wood alternates between wet and drier conditions.

Webster's Dictionary adds to the above description:

Somewhat like Longhorn beetles. The adults are strikingly coloured and frequent flowers. The larvae feed on decaying wood.

CHAPTER VI

A FALSE START

———◆———

WHILE *SEA BREEZE* UNDERWENT RENOVATION and rejuvenation I had to make a plan for the following summer's voyage and to find a crew. There is no record of the boat's history since the time she ceased to be a working boat. She must have changed owners frequently but I have no reason to believe that she had ever sailed outside home waters. It is never too late to start. All waters come alike to pilot cutters and there would certainly be no need to break her in gently by limiting our first season together to a series of trial runs in the frequented waters of the British Isles. A trial run might as well be a real trial and what better place for that than the North Atlantic and the Greenland Sea?

Obviously a return match with Jan Mayen had its attraction, but apart from thus tempting Providence rather blatantly I doubted whether we should be altogether welcome having so recently made a nuisance of ourselves. No such objection applied to Scoresby Sound which was still no more than a name to me and which could be reached without going anywhere near Jan Mayen. We could call again at the Faeroes and Iceland, preferably at some port other than Akureyri so as to provide a little variety. Thus it would be all new ground, Scoresby Sound excitingly new, and if we failed to reach it on account of ice we could retreat south to Angmagssalik to at least make sure of landing somewhere in Greenland.

Starting all over again with a new boat meant that I was faced with an uphill task, and on top of that was the finding of a crew without any nucleus round which to build. Living, while at home, in a remote part like a hermit, albeit in a pretty comfortable cell and not underfed, I have no large circle of friends and acquaintances through whom to put out feelers; while diffidence, or idleness, makes me unwilling to write and canvass possible sources such as universities, youth organisations, or even yacht clubs. Sitting back and waiting for sea-going enthusiasts

71

to write to me has the dubious merit of sparing me the trouble of having to choose. The number who write are seldom more than the number required; should they happen to be less I have to bestir myself. The critical might well say that the man gets the crews he deserves.

Quite early that winter a letter came from a Mike Brocklebank who had heard rumours of *Sea Breeze* and wished to volunteer his services. He showed he was serious by adding that since leave of absence would not be forthcoming he would have to give notice in good time. His job was to teach mechanical engineering at a secondary school: he was interested in boats, sailing, rock climbing, and had spent two years in the Corps of Signals. Teaching is not necessarily the same thing as doing but I felt that he would be well able to look after a small diesel engine. To me our Kermath diesel engine was a bit of an unknown quantity; so far it had lurked behind the companion-way ladder untroubled and unquestioned by John Tew, by me, or by anyone else. I met Mike at Chester and accepted him as the first recruit. He was thirty-two, single, strong, and enthusiastic.

One thing leads to another, as they say. A colleague of Mike's who taught woodwork at the same school now wanted to come too. I seemed to be off to a flying start—two tradesmen volunteers almost before I could look round. Again I went to Chester, a convenient halfway point, to meet Ralph Furness. Except that we met in the car-park instead of in a pub I felt like that Lieutenant Ayscough recruiting naval seamen in 1770 whose recruiting poster invited 'All true-blue British Hearts of Oak to repair to the Roundabout Tavern, Wapping, where he would be damn'd happy to shake hands with any old shipmates or their jolly Friends in general—Keep it up, my Boys—Twenty may play as well as one.' And in very small print below this warm invitation:

'For the encouragement of Discovering seamen, that they may be impressed, a reward of Two pounds will be given...' Ralph, though rather stout for a young man—a fault that a voyage in *Sea Breeze* would correct—seemed otherwise fit and a suitable candidate. My own woodworking talent extends little further than what in Africa we used to call bush-carpentry. In *Sea Breeze* a lot of new fittings would be needed below and Ralph would be the man to do them. He came from the Isle of Man and had messed about in boats.

My next recruit, whom I got through a mutual friend, was as old again as these two and of a very different occupation, being a retired bank manager. As such he inspired confidence at first sight, as all bank managers should, though in the case of Brian Potter it was not so much that he would not rob the till as that in no circumstances would he let a man down. He was big and burly and had kept himself fit by climbing, ski-ing, and canoeing. He had not the slightest experience of sailing or of small boats, yet I felt that my friend Lieutenant Ayscough at the Roundabout Tavern would have given two pounds for him on the nod. He offered to come as cook despite the fact that his cooking experience was little greater, extending no further than camp cooking, the sort that is done on a mountain or on the way to the mountains. Nor would his banking experience stand him in good stead at sea, but he had one valuable asset having been for many years an amateur cabinet-maker.

To meet him I had to make a wide deviation from the rhumb-line course from Barmouth to High Wycombe where Brian lived. It proved to be well worth while for I saw there his workshop and the furniture he had made—most of that in the house — and I came away thinking that carpenter Ralph would have little to do beyond handing tools to the maestro. From sales and junk-yards he collected Victorian pieces such as gigantic mahogany wardrobes which he would take to pieces and use in the making of reproductions of antique cabinets, tables, chairs. Brian, a married man with small grandchildren, had always allowed himself freedom to roam. Mrs Potter encouraged these numerous excursions abroad, or at least allowed him to decide whether all or any of these journeys were really necessary. As she told me, in the course of their lives she had on several occasions given Brian advice or directions that, having been reluctantly taken, had invariably turned out wrong. As Sancho Panza said, 'A wife's council is bad, but he who does not take it is mad.'

Finally, from information received, as the police say, I wrote to John Murray, an instructor (more teaching) at an adventure centre; the information coming, by the way, from Mike Brocklebank who did not know John but knew of him. After an exchange of letters John proved keen to come and we met at Lymington. The necessary leave of four months had been readily obtained, as indeed it ought to have been from a place devoted to fostering the spirit of adventure. He appeared neat, almost dapper, an appearance that struck with more stunning force as being in contrast with my own. He looked fit and agile, evidently a useful man aloft, as indeed he proved. We met on board *Sea Breeze* in the early spring when she was not looking her best, looking rather like a building site with the builders on strike. Even so she inspired confidence and John liked the look of her. As well as being a climber he knew a lot about boats and had sailed in most varieties with the exception of gaff-rigged boats. Thus it seemed to me I had a crew of all the talents; like the ministry of that name which, if I remember history rightly, had a short life.

Since we were not going to Jan Mayen and it would be of no avail arriving off Scoresby Sound until the end of July at the earliest, I decided to sail about mid-June. There was still a great deal of work to be done that the crew could do, far more, of course, than would have been called for in *Mischief*. The crew therefore assembled at the beginning of June, John bringing with him to help a lad from the adventure centre who made himself useful. The standing rigging was in order except that the forestay, a piece of wire even thicker than *Mischief*'s notoriously thick forestay, had needed shortening in order to fit to an equally massive rigging screw at the stemhead. Similarly with the topmast forestay, except that that was of wire of a size that an amateur could shorten and splice. The ratlines on the shrouds had to be renewed, a job that had to be done first so that we could get aloft. The old lanyards, stiff with tar and hard as iron, had had to be cut, probably with a hacksaw, when the mast had been taken out. New lanyards of Italian hemp—not easily found in these synthetic times—had to be rove and for this I had the help of Ted Mapes, an old sailor and formerly bosun of the yard. By means of tackles and plenty of tallow we got them pretty tight. Whether old shellbacks would approve I can't say, but the best way to get lanyards really tight is to set them up under sail. The lee side shrouds being slack their lanyards are easily set up good and tight, and the other side are similarly done when on the other tack.

During the winter I had taken home all the running rigging for overhauling; it remained merely to discover where it all went, hang and reeve the blocks, and to make sure that the numerous halyards were leading fair and not chafing. The last is the most important and the hardest to achieve. Those peak and throat chain halyards that I had abolished would, of course, have laughed at chafe, but it would have been worse than unseamanlike to hoist the mainsail with the engine while the crew looked on admiringly. After her first three voyages we had sailed *Mischief* without a topmast, detracting a little from her appearance and not much from her performance. The topsail that the topmast enables one to set is always the first sail to come down when the wind freshens and in the North Atlantic, even in mid-summer, it would not often be set. And what with the topsail sheet and halyards, the topmast's shrouds and backstays, and the tackle for lowering the topmast, the gear aloft is almost doubled, involving more care and maintenance and muddling the minds of a strange crew. The slender spar on *Sea Breeze* certainly added to her good looks and I felt so proud of these good looks that I decided to leave the topmast up and await the event. Compared with her mainmast it looked like a toothpick and in the words of Mr Chucks the bosun 'precarious and not at all permanent'. My correspondent Mr England tells me that in her working day she had a pole-mast, that is, a mast of the same height but in one piece.

Having spent so much already I could not afford any alterations below. Except for the removal of doors, carpets, and curtains, the accommodation remained as before. A sail rack had been built forward in the peak and on one side of the galley a chart table, still leaving the whole of the port side as the cook's domain. The engine, too, is at the after end of the galley behind the steps leading up into the cockpit where it is remarkably inaccessible. An old Lymington friend of mine, Sandy Lee, wanted to improve the companion-way ladder. The steps were awkwardly placed and it was too functional for his aesthetic eye. He made a new one of oak with a pleasing curve, so well-designed that a blind man could climb up without missing a step or hitting his head on the sliding hatch above. Thus in effect I had three craftsmen embellishing *Sea Breeze*, or say two craftsmen and a carpenter.

Many shelves were needed, shelves over the foot of each bunk for personal gear, shelves for books, barograph, and wireless set, racks for charts, bottles, and tumblers, and a removable fiddle for the saloon table. With the abolition of the gas stove the entire re-arrangement of the galley fittings and shelves gave Brian plenty of scope even if the standard of work required and the time available meant rough carpentry instead of cabinet making. Mike did us a good turn by retrieving from a dump a discarded vice, still serviceable and amply big enough. The boat already had a substantial work-bench up forward where we could mount it and where queues began forming up to make use of it.

All the electric wiring had to be renewed, the plumbing rearranged, and a new whale pump added to supplement a pump driven off the engine.

> To furnish a wife will cost you some trouble
> But to fit out a ship the expenses are double.

The fresh water was carried in four 30-gallon tanks underneath the two bunks in the saloon. They prevented any doubling up of the bunks and they proved devilish awkward to fill. With the original plumbing—and the replacement was not much better—unless you turned various cocks in the right sequence you might find that when all four tanks were supposedly full, three were still empty and the overflow from the fourth had flooded the saloon.

The ship's compass was very small and so far as one could see had been held in the hand while steering. *Mischief*'s compass had been mounted on the floor of her capacious cockpit where in *Sea Breeze* there was no room for it. The only place for it we could find was over the top of the companion-way hatch and the only type of compass that could be read at that height and distance away from the helmsman was a Sestrel. Mr Lee made a little bridge over the sliding hatch to mount it on and a brass cage to protect it from the knocks it might suffer in such an exposed position. Visitors to *Sea Breeze* are often puzzled by this sort of parrot cage so prominently displayed, and in the absence of any bird they take it to be some new-fangled radar device. This compass is marked in degrees instead of points, good enough for a steamer which is not much concerned with the wind but not for a sailing ship where the wind and its direction is all that matters. The wind direction is always named by the points of the compass and it is confusing to switch to degrees when ordering the course to be steered. To add to the confusion this type of compass is read from the back instead of the front, as it must be to be read at all by the helmsman, so that on an alteration of course one has to think twice before deciding which way to push the tiller. Like most things about a boat it is a compromise solution of what is desirable and what is possible, and I shall have to find another solution before throwing it overboard.

Before coming to the action, and to conclude this long-drawn tale of preparation, there is only a little to add. The boat's large and heavy dinghy, so heavy that it had to be launched from a davit, had also to be abolished, or at least I abolished the davit and swapped it for a lighter nine-foot dinghy. Owing to the great hydraulic winch we could find no room on the foredeck, so that even this smaller dinghy-had to be carried amidships where it cluttered up the deck and was much in the way of the jib and staysail sheets. Having seen enough of anthracite-burning stoves I reverted to a Kempsafe cabin heater that conveniently burns the same fuel as the engine. We had used one in *Mischief* and except for an occasional holocaust due to carelessness it had given no trouble. The skylight immediately above the stove has to be kept firmly closed, and even so has been known to let in water, and finding a suitable exit for the stove-pipe presented a problem. Engineer Mike's solution involved two right-angle bends and we lived to regret them.

We were not in all respects ready for sea until June 17th. The nearer the day came the more I wondered whether we were in all respects ready, for we were starting from scratch. Putting *Mischief* into commission after being laid-up for the winter was a simple matter; everything required was in the store on shore and had merely to be put in the right place on board. Now one had to think afresh of all that might be needed. Galley equipment, for instance, of which, with the boat, I had not inherited enough to stock a picnic basket. There were no tools of any kind, but happily for this voyage we were exceedingly well off because Brian, Mike, and Ralph all brought their own. Then there were all the bits and pieces that we were wont to carry, things that might never be used but without which one would not feel the boat was really well-found. Spare blocks, wire strops and grommets, short bits of chain, handy-billy, shackles, wire, rope, copper, canvas, bosun's stores of all kinds, and a hundred other items. But we were not sailing for some unknown shore and most of what a small boat may need can be readily found at the Faeroes or Iceland.

For reasons already given I never insured the boat for the voyage but I usually took the comparatively cheap precaution of insuring her while in home waters, these being the most dangerous. Mere prudence warns one to keep as far as possible from any steamers, especially from trawlers, yet wide as the sea is, ships frequently collide and yachts are occasionally run down. A graver risk for me in a big, heavy boat that is not as handy as a modern yacht, and that has fourteen feet of bowsprit sticking out ahead, was that of hitting another yacht. Lymington river is narrow and lined on both sides by expensive yachts lying at their moorings, and in one's anxiety to give the Lymington-Yarmouth ferry room to pass it would be all too easy to foul one of them. Or, perhaps, in the event of some unseamanlike behaviour by both parties, one might impale on the bowsprit some lofty gin-palace.

With all this in mind and a strange boat under me I took care when we cast off on June 17th to have Ted Mapes in a launch to escort us halfway down the river where the bends are narrowest and sharpest. As we passed the club-house of the Royal Lymington Yacht Club they gave us a starting gun, an encouraging gesture that we had long been honoured with in *Mischief.* Strong, blustery, south-westerly weather had prevailed for the last day or two, weather entirely unfavourable for beating down Channel in a strange boat with a strange crew. I had therefore decided to sail about in the Solent to see how she went and to anchor for the night in Yarmouth roads. Clear of the river but before we had begun hoisting any sails I noticed a lot of water coming into the galley high up on the starboard side, and on removing a bit of the lining we enjoyed a view of the Isle of Wight between two of the waterline planks where a foot or two of caulking had spewed out.

Having anchored in the roads I went ashore to see the harbourmaster and to inform the yard at Lymington. We then moved inside the harbour preparatory to leaning the boat against the quayside wall towards midnight when the tide served. By mid-June Yarmouth harbour is bursting at the seams and manoeuvring *Sea Breeze* into her allotted berth shook my weak nerves. How thankful I was for that insurance policy. The ornate gangway of a large Royal Yacht Squadron power boat narrowly escaped destruction at our hands, and the crew of the yacht lying ahead of our mooring must have thought their time had come.

Later on a wet and windy night we were towed alongside the quay and at high tide we turned out to haul the boat forward and heel her over by swinging out the boom. Early in the morning the yard launch came over with two men who recaulked the planks. We had yet to see the sails hoisted and since the weather remained too discouraging to start we went out into the Solent to hoist them. The boat sailed well, went about with no fuss, and after two hours sailing, mostly hard on the wind, we returned to the anchorage well pleased with her performance. But there seemed to be a lot of water in the well, and by the time I had given it 600 strokes I felt something akin to despair. After all the time and money that had been spent the boat was obviously in no condition to take to sea. After more telephone consultation with the yard we repeated the performance of the previous night, laying her once more against the quay wall. In the morning quite a party arrived early enough for a cup of tea—John Tew and the yard manager with their attendants.

After inspecting the hull John Tew's verdict was that the boat must be recaulked throughout. The weather being what it was we had so far lost nothing, but it maddened me to think of the boat lying all that winter in a shed and that no one—neither John Tew, the yard, nor the owner—had had the gumption to examine the caulking. In defence all that could be said was that it looked sound, that the boat had made no water on passage from the Hamble, and had remained dry when put back in the water in the spring. But an hour's sailing in the quiet waters of the Solent had soon found out the rottenness of the caulking. By June 20th she was back at Lymington once more hauled out on the slip. The crew dispersed to foregather again in a week's time.

CHAPTER VII

SECOND AND THIRD START

———————————◆———————————

T HIS DISCOURAGING, COSTLY SETBACK had at least occurred at the right time, before the voyage had even begun. If any of the crew were given to conjecture they could exercise it by wondering what might have happened had the caulking started coming out in chunks when we were on our way and far from land. In order to lessen the windage aloft while the boat was in the cradle on the slip we had sent down the topmast. By June 30th, the topmast once more set up, we were ready for a fresh start. In far more genial weather we beat out through the Needles Channel, sighting a Thames barge under sail and a Dutch botter, the three of us the only sailing vessels about. In the past week at home Brian must have made some study of an art new to him, surprising us all by serving up curry and a noble duff on our first night at sea.

Fitful winds by day and windless nights made for slow, peaceful progress until July 4th when we made a run of ninety-five miles that took us somewhere south-east of the Scillies. With both genoa and tops'l set, the topmast bending like a fishing rod, I took fright and had both sails taken down. Five days out and we had not yet rounded Land's End. Next afternoon in thick weather and a near gale we sighted Round Island at the north end of the Scillies and had to go about to weather it. Close reefed and with no jib set, we tacked again at nightfall to weather Cape Cornwall, the small jib having blown out when Mike inadvertently let the sheet fly. We spent a wet night, close-hauled, just maintaining our distance from the Cornish coast and a lee shore. The more or less halcyon days and nights spent drifting down Channel had not prepared the crew for the rough usage of the last two days when they found that yachting had pains as well as pleasures. They were far from well and the boat proved decidedly wet. She needed 500 strokes of the pump every watch though most of this water found its way below from the deck. The beam in the galley dripped generously over Brian

SECOND AND THIRD START

and the chart table, as did the beam in way of the mast, wetting my bunk on the one tack and Brian's on the other. Another source of water was the stern gland which later John succeeded in tightening. But in the last windy twenty-four hours the boat had logged 146 miles. We were well pleased with her sailing ability and the way she went about in rough water even when close-reefed, never once missing stays as *Mischief* had sometimes done, obliging us to put her about by gybing.

Brian, the landsman, alone remained unaffected by the weather and seemed to be the only one of the crew enjoying life. He was never idle, which is perhaps half the secret, always having in hand some carpentry job in addition to normal work in the galley. With such a crew to help he preferred to do his own washing-up. The crew usually take turns as galley-slave, washing-up, drawing sea-water for the cook, peeling spuds, and cleaning up below deck. John at least knew what had to be done and was almost too enthusiastic about keeping things below sweet and clean by generous swabbing down. Had we had the means I could see him wanting to smoke the boat out to ward off incipient scurvy.

The crew had a welcome respite in smooth water when we passed close under the lee of Lundy Island. Off Lundy we sighted the royal yacht *Britannia*. I had last seen her at Reykjavik in 1964 when *Mischief*, the only British vessel in harbour, had sailed out to pay her respects as *Britannia* steamed in with the Duke of Edinburgh on board. With the wind still at north-west we held on northwards until midnight of July 8th when we raised the light of the lightship off Worm Head west of Swansea. Upon the new heading of slightly south of west the boat began to pitch heavily in a short, steep sea. It must have been this violent pitching that brought down the topmast. I had barely settled down in the cockpit at 4 a.m. when with a loud crack the topmast went, a bit of it caressing me lightly on the head as it fell on the deck nearby. A minute or two later I realised that the bowsprit, too, had gone. Without the topmast forestay and with no jib set it was no longer supported. All hands were called to clear the wreckage. Using the jib halyards we first got the bowsprit inboard, for it had broken at the gammon iron and was bashing against the hull. A large piece of the topmast hung athwart the main forestay in a tangle of wire and rope, shrouds and halyards. Working from a bosun's chair shackled to the forestay John at length had it all down.

The topmast could be regarded as expendable but the bowsprit was indispensable. We were well placed for making Appledore, only twenty-five miles down wind, so with a fine sailing breeze we eased away the main sheet and let her rip. There is a bar across the entrance to Appledore and we had the tide to catch. Having no large-scale chart we had to follow carefully the directions in the Pilot and as soon as we had picked up the bar buoy found it all plain sailing. The two Customs officers who presently boarded us did not allow sympathy for our mishap to overcome their duty of sealing up our bonded store locker. The tides were at neaps with not enough water for us to lie alongside the wall. We had to anchor out in the river where even the neap tides run with great strength. Having put the Customs officers ashore in our dinghy, and getting them thoroughly wet, I sought out Messrs Hinks boatyard to put in hand a new bowsprit.

This small yard had recently completed the building of *Nonsuch*, a replica of the seventeenth-century ship whose voyage in 1668 had marked the founding of the Hudson Bay Company. In 1668 two French traders, De Groseilliers and Radisson, supported and financed by Prince Rupert (cousin of Charles II) and his friends, sailed for Hudson Bay in two small ships, *Nonsuch* and *Eaglet*. Storm damage forced *Eaglet* to turn back but the *Nonsuch* under Captain Zacharia Hillam reached the mouth of Rupert River and wintered there. When they returned to England the next year with a fortune in furs on board, the Hudson Bay region, hitherto explored only in the hope of finding a north-west passage, became attractive in its own right. In 1670, under the patronage of Prince Rupert, the Hudson Bay Company was founded, and received a charter giving it almost sovereign rights over all lands whose waters drained into Hudson Bay. It was to celebrate this tricentenary that the *Nonsuch* had been built for the Hudson Bay Company who intended her to sail across the Atlantic to take part in the celebrations. She had proved a bit tender for an Atlantic voyage and in the end was shipped over in a freighter.

The yard had no timber long enough for the bowsprit and had to order it from St Austell. On arrival the timber turned out to be twenty-four feet long instead of twenty-five feet, but to avoid delay I accepted the shorter length even though it meant our having to make up new bowsprit shrouds. By July 10th the tides had made sufficiently for us

Sea Breeze setting out, as seen from Hurst Point *(Photo: W. G. Lee)*

to go alongside the wall, a change much to the better. Except at slack
water, rowing ashore was difficult. If the dinghy were laden, the per-
spiring oarsman might finish up half a mile below or above the point
aimed at. At low water alongside the wall we had a chance to examine
the hull and found it in good shape except for a bit of stopping that
had come out near the stem. We had a line from the mast to the wall
to prevent her falling over as the tide dropped, and once or twice we
would either forget to shorten up the line as the boat took the ground
and began to lean over away from the wall, or to slack away as the boat
rose at high tide. On these occasions a loud warning cry testified to
the professional alertness of the old salts who spent their days on the
quay regarding and criticising the passing nautical scene. Were they
thinking:

> How pleasant to gaze on the sailors
> To gaze without having to sail.

Among the trippers and retired seafarers who kept an eye on *Sea Breeze*
was Captain Jewel, lately owner and master of a beautiful three-masted
trading schooner *Kathleen and May*. At least ten years before, on a visit
to Appledore by land, I had seen the schooner lying alongside and
had admired the yacht-like fashion in which this trading vessel was
maintained. *Kathleen and May* was now lying up the river towards Bideford, laid-up but not neglected. I went on board and as I gazed up at
her lofty spars I was not surprised when the present owner told me it
had taken him two months single-handed to scrape down and varnish
those three tall masts. I had a word with Captain Jewel who remarked
on the absence of our topmast and considered it a grave mistake to sail,
as we intended, without one. For his part, he said, he would sooner sail
without a bowsprit.

On the 12th men from the yard wheeled our bowsprit along and
lowered it over the wall for us to reeve. It went in with less trouble
than I had expected and we could then measure the length for the new
bowsprit shrouds and for a new stay from the masthead to the cranse
iron at the end of the bowsprit. Turning in a splice in plough-steel wire
takes time so that it is important to get the measurements right.

By now I had other things to think about as well. The two school-
masters had decided to quit. Mike had heard at second hand that his

mother was ill, and although we urged him to get some reliable information, say from a doctor, he merely said he ought to go home. Ralph lingered, idle and sulky, while he made up his mind and then he likewise departed. It seemed that their early experiences had fallen short of their expectations. So much had gone wrong since first leaving Lymington that they may have likened *Sea Breeze* to Milton's

> Fatal and perfidious bark,
> Built in th' eclipse, and rigged with curses dark.

At times I had been tempted to think the same.

Here was a facer. I had no reserves to call up; either we must find two local volunteers or expect a delay of several weeks and the consequent abandonment of most of our plans. John remained staunch and full of hope in spite of this latest and worst setback, while Brian I knew was not the man to stop stirring till the pudding was done. Surely, I thought, in Appledore or Bideford, home of Sir Richard Grenville, not to mention *Westward Ho* and all that that implied, the spirit of adventurous seafaring must still flourish. The first likely covert to draw seemed to be the North Devon Yacht Club at Instow across the river to which I now went by ferry. Keen racing men they were, no doubt, but a little parochial. I could forgive them for never having heard of *Mischief*, but whence we had come, Lymington, and whither we were bound, Greenland, were equally beyond their ken. Even the magic word 'the Solent', the yachtsman's Mecca, roused no flicker of interest in these Devon infidels. One of the youngest members did indeed seem momentarily to catch fire at the mention of Greenland, but unluckily mother was at hand to stamp it out.

Nevertheless this Instow visit bore fruit. The boatman who ferried me over—our needs were now common knowledge—gave me the name of a Welshman, an intruder on the Devon scene, whom he thought might come. Dai Morgan, or Ken as he was rightly called, was living in a caravan pending the renovation of a nearby cottage that he had bought. He was doing everything himself, brickwork, plumbing, heating, lighting, glazing, the lot—evidently a king among handymen. He had been an agricultural engineer in South Wales and had now retired to Appledore having conceived no great love for his own countrymen. Besides a lifetime's experience of engines he had a great liking for the sea, had helped her present owner to bring *Kathleen and May* round from Southampton, and also to bring an old trading ketch to England from the Baltic.

On the debit side he was elderly, far from spry, and did not look robust. He would be no help on deck except for doing his two-hour trick at the helm if well wrapped up. Having had a look at *Sea Breeze* and talked to John and Brian he expressed his readiness to join. Readiness was the word. I could not but admire the carefree way in which he arranged his affairs for a three months' absence by putting together a few necessities, parking the cat with a neighbour, locking the caravan and the half-finished cottage, and repairing on board next day. As might have been expected, he proved of great value as engineer, methodical and painstaking to a degree, and withal a good shipmate, except that throughout the voyage, in spite of many disappointments, he always expected the worst to happen. To me he will always figure as Cassandra Ken.

The ripples from the stone cast at Instow spread. On the 13th a young man came along to see the boat and those in her, and promised to return that evening with a definite answer, which he did. Colin Kavenan had heard about us from a friend in the Yacht Club. He was at a loose end waiting to attend some course and could get himself ready by the next day, parents no obstacle. He had done some boating and was a keen fisherman. Colin wore a beard, but at this crisis in our affairs I would not have minded had he worn beads and had hair down to his waist. Thus in a week after putting into Appledore we had a new bowsprit fitted and had replaced our two deserters with rather more promising material; and unless another spar carried away pretty soon, a change of mind on their part would be of no avail.

It was late on the evening of the 15th before we cast off. We had had to cut some links out of the bobstay chain in order to get it bar taut, and Ken and Colin had some last minute arrangements to make. The following morning in poor visibility the Smalls lighthouse appeared as expected, a feat that I attributed more to luck than to good navigation. With the Bristol Channel to the east and St George's Channel to the north the tidal streams hereabouts are both strong and complex, owing apparently to the difficulty the stream has in deciding into which of the two channels it should be running. The *Pilot* devotes five pages to the subject and to hoist it all in requires a clearer head than mine. *Sea*

Breeze seemed bent on making up lost time by reeling off over ninety miles to pass the Codling light vessel next day. We had Snowdon in sight, nearly sixty miles away, and for supper, mackerel with cheese sauce and a treacle duff. Colin had brought a short spinning rod. If there were mackerel about, and he seemed to know when they were, he would catch them.

A falling glass and a southerly wind presaged some wet, windy weather. In order to get well clear of the Irish coast we ran off to the north-east, and a great dollop of water through the skylight hinted that the sea was becoming rough. In the course of the voyage we tried various dodges with the skylight, making it more water-tight but never quite waterproof; if a sea hit the skylight coaming with any force it always managed to lift the skylight just enough for a jet of water to burst through. The place of honour—the head of the table where the skipper sat—was, as it should be, the place of danger. Later that afternoon in heavy rain and poor visibility we hove to as we were rapidly closing the Isle of Man. Between squalls we sighted the island and started sailing, the plan being to run up the coast to the north until we had a good lee and smoother water in which to gybe the boat round. Off Point of Ayr we were in relatively calm water and should have stayed there. Clear of the land, conditions became so bad that I decided to heave to for the night. In strong winds it is almost impossible to keep oil-burning navigation lamps alight, and ours were probably out when we had an alarmingly close shave with a small tanker. When the tanker stood on in spite of a powerful torch directed at him we hastily let draw and gybed away so that he passed some fifty yards off. Perhaps the trick of making oil lamps wind-proof is no longer known. A hundred or even fifty years ago, when oil lamps were in common use at sea, it is hard to believe that a gale of wind would promptly extinguish them all.

In more moderate weather we made rapid progress, sighting the Maidens north of Belfast the next evening. On the previous windy night even Brian had had to restrict supper to soup and bully beef sandwiches, and to give him a chance to make up for this with a curry, as well as to cheat an adverse tide, we anchored once again in Red Bay. Sailing after lunch next day, wind and tide both in our favour, we were soon off Rathlin Island. As we sailed by close to the shore Colin stood by, rod in hand, and on seeing what he judged to be a fishy-looking eddy made a cast and hauled out four huge mackerel at one go. Originally we had intended calling at the Faeroes where my Danish friend in *Ole Roemer* would be. We were a month late; *Ole Roemer* by now would probably be on her way to Scoresby Sound, so I decided to sail direct to Iceland. Accordingly, when south of Skerryvore, we headed northwest out into the Atlantic where we enjoyed fine weather and fast sailing. The fine weather lasted only two days but for the next six days we ran over 100 miles a day. Even on the 25th, when we were hove to for several hours during a southerly gale, we still made good our 100 miles. When hove to, we found that the boat forged ahead much too fast, mainly because, unlike *Mischief*, there were no sheet winches and it was hard to haul the staysail flat aback. Later, to correct this, we used a tackle. Macaroni cheese and treacle duff for supper.

On this headlong rush towards Iceland we got too far south and fetched up in the vicinity of Hvalbakur, or Whale-back Island, only sixteen feet high, twenty-five miles out from the land, and, of course, unlit. In approaching this east coast one needs to be wary on account, as the Pilot stresses, of the off-lying streams, and the unreliability of the magnetic compass when near the land. One reason for our having picked on Seydisfjord for our landfall was its freedom from off-lying dangers and we had no business to be closing the land when still forty miles to the south. Having steered north we headed in again on what I thought was the right latitude, but a snap meridian sight, the sun having been for the most part hidden, showed that we were still to the southward. Under the lee of Iceland, in a region of prevailing Westerlies, one would expect to find pretty smooth water. Not a bit. The nearer we approached the land the more lumpy and irregular the sea became owing, no doubt, to strong tidal streams.

On July 28th, after another southerly gale and in a horribly confused sea, as we steered gingerly towards the land, visibility grew worse and worse. At midnight, when it was down to about two cables, we altered course to the north, roughly parallel to the coast, my frayed nerves unable to stand it any longer. Ken had been on watch but being ill-clad and feeling the cold he had had to be relieved. We had done well to alter course. Shortly after I had taken over something more solid than the fog loomed close on our port, the vague outline of a high island. From the description in the *Pilot* I took it to be Skrudhur, 520 feet high: 'This islet is an excellent landmark, both on account of its shape and of its height, as all the other islets on this part of the coast are low.' It was then too late, but had we known earlier that we were in its vicinity more attention might have been paid to the remarks in the *Pilot* about local magnetic anomalies:

> Eastward and southward of Skrudhur the compass is especially affected, the greatest observed anomaly being 22°E. in a position 3 to 4 miles south-eastward of the island; three-quarters of a mile northward of this position the anomaly was 11°W., and it ceased altogether a quarter of a mile southward of the position. About 4¾ miles eastward of Skrudhur an anomaly of 17°E. has been observed, and between Skrudhur and the mainland, one of 11°E.

Such large anomalies could hardly be called niceties of navigation, but in a small sailing boat, where precise navigation is hardly possible, content as one is to steer within half a point or so of a given course, they would generally be disregarded. No wonder that in the days of sail before happenings as strange as these had been observed and recorded for the benefit of sailors, every stress was laid on what they called the four L's—lead, log, latitude, and look-out, the last being the ultimate safeguard on which all depends.

When the wind died away to nothing and the gaff began to jerk wildly as the boat tossed about in the confused sea, I took the extreme step of calling all hands well before breakfast to hand the mainsail. Then she really began to dance about but with no longer the chance of doing herself any harm. Brian, always on a level with circumstances, cooked the usual breakfast porridge, and by the time that was finished we had the land in sight. The sea quietened down and with the dispersal of the fog I could check by sights that the island we had seen was undoubtedly Skrudhur. With no wind and twenty miles to go to Dalatangi lighthouse at the entrance to our fjord we started the engine. It had been a remarkably fast passage. In eleven days from Appledore to Iceland we had covered 1,083 miles. We did nothing like as well on the homeward run, or indeed on the voyage the following year. On long passages I found it wise to count on nothing better than seventy miles a day.

CHAPTER VIII

A POLITE MUTINY
OFF THE GREENLAND COAST

THE PORT OF BUDHAREYRI at the head of Seydisfjordhur, whither we were bound, is thus described in the Pilot: 'The town contains a hotel with fifteen beds, and numerous fish-filleting, freezing, and fish-oil factories. There are fifteen piers and jetties.' Naturally we expected to see a busy, thriving port, perhaps with a Seaman's Home like that at Reykjavik where meals can be had, but these expectations had to be modified. Upon reaching the place one could tell at once that it was far from busy, in fact almost moribund. The departure of the herring from Iceland waters has changed things here as on the north coast, but unlike Akureyri there is no farming in this region and no tourists, so that Budhareyri has been hard hit. The hotel was closed, only one fish factory worked part time, and the piers and jetties were largely deserted. A Customs officer who came on board advised us to move to another part of the harbour where we lay in solitary state at a quay long enough, if not deep enough, to accommodate the Queen Mary.

Having reached Iceland in spite of so many setbacks I began to think that Scoresby Sound was in the bag, but even as we chugged quietly up the fjord these sanguine hopes received a jolt. John, who for the past week had complained of being ill, having perked up on reaching the calm waters of the fjord, chose that moment to hint that we had come far enough; but considering the weakness of the crew and his own infirmity, we would do well, after perhaps seeing something more of Iceland, to start for home. Naturally I could not agree to that and told him that we would push on as far as we could and that I could judge for myself when the time had come to turn back. He attributed his illness to those unlucky mackerel caught off Rathlin Island, a fish to which, he said, he was allergic. There was talk of seeing a doctor as soon as we arrived at Budhareyri, but having arrived he said no more about his health and consulted no doctor.

For all the depressingly dull, wet weather, so unlike what we had experienced at Akureyri, we enjoyed our stay. The natives regarded us with friendly amusement, a provincial paper having recorded our advent under the unkind headlines 'Old men in an Old Boat'. We made good use of some communal shower baths and began finding our way around. There was no High Street or shopping centre. The shops were of a retiring nature, looking like private houses, and had to be searched for. Local knowledge was indispensable. At a shop like an old-fashioned draper's Ken and Colin found all they lacked in the way of thick sweaters, wool shirts, long pants, and even oilskins. There was a well-stocked liquor store selling every kind of spirit from whisky to Black Death. The Iceland authorities regard beer, rather than gin, as the original Mother's Ruin. The only beer permitted is the non-alcoholic variety brewed by the state brewery with Black Death as a profitable by-product. Brian, who believes in and practises living off the country, treated himself to a bottle. It tastes like surgical spirit laced with aniseed.

The parson of the Lutheran church was a surprising and amusing visitor. He arrived just as we were having our tea, and having laced his tea with whisky from a bottle that emerged unobtrusively from a pocket as if by a conjuring trick, between puffs from a cigar, he devoured with relish biscuits well spread with jam. He had spent three years in London, spoke idiomatic English and appeared exceedingly well-informed. In return we were invited the next evening to the Manse or its Lutheran equivalent where, though a little hampered by the attentions of the parson's seven children, we set about a fine array of cakes, savouries, biscuits, and some notable shrimp mayonnaise. Coffee, of course, with endless doses of Black Death in small glasses accompanied by the usual 'Skolls'. Another guest was the manager of the fish factory from whom we hoped to elicit the solution to the herring mystery. His explanation, confused by indifferent English and too much Black Death, was that the mature herring, having learnt sense, swim low and escape the nets, while the inexperienced young, the breeding stock of the future, are caught. Anyway over-fishing had finished off the Iceland herring.

We returned late from the party in driving rain and a wind so strong that before turning in I put out more warps. Brian and I resolved to climb Strandertinder (3310 feet), the peak that towers in modest fashion over the town. The rain that had been falling since the previous night let up towards evening allowing us to set off. Starting right from sea-level, scratch as it were, we had every foot of it to climb, a long slog that took two hours and a half. The extensive view from the top suffered from sameness, all the surrounding mountains appearing much the same size and shape. We found a better way down where patches of surviving winter snow gave us some long glissades.

Sea Breeze has two port-holes, one in the saloon and one in my cabin. It was usually under water and I never really became accustomed to watching all that green water surging by, separated from it by only a small piece of glass.

> When the cabin port-holes are dark and green
> Because of the seas outside;
> When the steward falls into the soup tureen
> And the chairs begin to slide.
> Why then you may know if you haven't guessed
> That you're fifty north and forty west.

But the fear that they might be broken by a stray piece of ice was really what decided me to cover them with an iron plate outside, a dead-light. The stove pipe also needed a cowl and when that had been fitted we tried the stove. In port, where there is no down-draught from the mainsail, it burnt well despite the two bends in the pipe.

By Saturday, August 2nd, having set up and tarred the lanyards, filled up with water, paraffin, sixty gallons of diesel oil, and black bread, we were ready to go. John had said no more about cutting short the voyage and I assumed, with reservations, that all was well. That I was not over-hopeful is confirmed by an entry in my brief diary— 'wonder how far we shall get?' Much depended on what we met in the way of weather. Outside the fjord we picked up a north-easterly breeze and were able to lay a course that would take us well clear of the Langanes Peninsula. But next day the wind veered south-east bringing with it the fog that was to persist more or less continuously for the next five days. We were still making too much water, 600 strokes of the pump every watch to clear the bilge, until John had another go at the stern gland when the number of strokes required fell to 100. Until then he had been gloomy but after being sick as a result of crawling under the counter he brightened up a lot. That night after a supper of macaroni, hash, peas, and a sad but nevertheless satisfying duff we crossed the Arctic circle. No ceremonies, no sky-larking, no visit from 'Le Père Arctique' marked the occasion.

In spite of a backing of the wind on the next day to north of east, the thick, wet fog lay heavily over the sea as if part of it. Indeed one found it hard to determine where the one began and the other ended. Fog, as the Pilot notes, is more likely with southerly winds, but there can be no cast-iron rules for the insidious comings and goings of this depressing frequenter of northern waters:

> During the summer, when gales are rare and the wind is generally light, fog is often widespread and persistent. It sometimes continues for days or even weeks... Fogs are most general with winds from some southerly point; with northerly or north-westerly winds they usually disperse, although sometimes persisting for several hours after a shift of wind northward following a long spell of southerly winds.

It began to get cold, the air temperature 41° F. and the sea down to 38° F., high time for long woolly pants and vests. Combined with the fog it had a discouraging effect upon a far from eager crew and the refusal of the stove to burn properly did not mend matters. Ken decided that the right-angle bends must be eliminated, and together with John set to work as though their lives depended on it. They effected a great improvement though the cowl had still to be carefully trimmed according to the wind. Renewed mutterings came from John who until our arrival in Iceland had struck me as entirely reliable, the last man to want to quit, and one of the best mates I had had. How much longer did I propose bumbling about the Arctic in thick fog with a weak crew, no communication with anybody, no variety in the food, and himself unfit? For supper that night, a melancholy feast, we had sausages, cabbage, and a prime treacle duff.

On the morning of the 6th, after some heavy rain, a northerly wind sprang up. Obeying the rules, for once the fog became less dense and our horizon widened. Unfortunately the sun remained obstinately hidden and no sights could be obtained. We sailed fast for most of the day and at 6 p.m., when I took the sea temperature for entry in the meteorological log, it had fallen to 32° F. The hint that ice could not be far off was confirmed a little later when we sighted a small berg. More scattered floes appeared, the flotsam and jetsam of the main pack, and at 7 p.m. we hove to. The sighting of ice caused John concern though, as I pointed out, anyone who embarks on a voyage to the Arctic would expect to see something of the sort sooner or later.

I should have been happier myself had we known where we were. For four days we had had no sights and this meeting with the ice showed that the coast could not be far away. Our respite from fog did not last long. But next day, for a change, the sun shone brightly while the fog returned as thick as ever—a shallow fog with blue sky overhead. To have a sun and no horizon is far more maddening than to have no sun at all. In desperation I brought the sun down on to the back of a fulmar sitting on the water a 100 yards from the ship and directly under the sun. After making due allowance for height of eye, height of fulmar, etc., the sight when worked out put us well up on the Greenland ice-cap.

August 8th is a day I always remember. It was our black day in 1970 just as it had been Hindenberg's black day in 1918, on which the unit I was happy to be with played an active part. With a light easterly breeze we had sailed quietly all night until the morning when the wind backed north and began to freshen. As the fog slowly thinned we sighted first pack-ice to the east. Then suddenly, like the raising of a curtain, the fog dissolved and we were gazing with astonishment at a wild, mountainous coastline stretching far into the distance on either hand. After having been more or less blindfold for so long it seemed to me more like a revelation than a landfall. Directly opposite were two big glaciers, evidently descending from the ice-cap, for the mountains in the vicinity carried remarkably little snow. A cluster of jagged pinnacles far to the south stood out black against the morning sky.

What a time one could have, I thought, poking about in those numerous, largely unknown fjords if one could only reach them, forgetting that if it were not for the ever-present ice they would not have remained so long unknown. To the north-east the coast seemed to terminate in a cape twenty to twenty-five miles away. A hasty sight taken from an assumed position fifteen miles from the coast gave me a clue and comparing the lie of the land with the chart I took this cape to be Cape Brewster at the southern entrance to Scoresby Sound. Instead of an unbroken mass the pack-ice seemed to lie in scattered fields and my hopes began to rise. Sailing north in increasing wind we soon came up with one of these fields and turned in towards the coast in the hope of finding a lead.

Rain now accompanied the rising wind. Intent on seizing the chance that our first fog-free day had given us, thinking the barograph had risen whereas in fact it had begun to fall, I did not pay much heed to these warnings. As Lecky says: 'A falling barometer with a northerly wind conveys a warning that cannot be disregarded with impunity.' Upon meeting more ice we followed its edge to the north-west but were always confronted by more ice ahead. By this time, late afternoon, the wind looked like increasing to a gale and the rain fairly pelted down; but the sea remained perfectly smooth thanks to the protecting fields of ice that almost surrounded us. Under the engine, I thought, the ice might well be navigable. The question was whether to try it here or to go out to sea clear of the ice and make the latitude of Scoresby Sound before attempting to reach the coast. The last would probably be the better course, but meantime we could heave to where we were in calm water and wait for the wind to abate. Between the widely scattered fields there would be room to keep well away from any ice.

John would have none of it. Like Brer Rabbit, in the language of Uncle Remus, he seemed to imagine that 'every minnit wuz gwineter be de nex'. In order to pacify him we began sailing east in search of open water. While running along the edge of some ice that seemed to stretch interminably southwards, looking for a break, and getting tired of losing so much ground to the south, I took the boat in close and real-ised that the ice was no field but a thin line of floes. We sailed through without difficulty and the roughness of the sea beyond showed that there was no ice to the north. Whereupon we hove to on the starboard tack to ride out the night. A dirty night it proved and I soon realised we had hove to on the wrong tack when the boat, by fore-reaching, brought us back within sight of the ice. We went about and lay to on the port tack heading east.

The rain stopped before morning but the wind continued to blow with some fury throughout the day. As I listened vainly for any lulls that might herald a lessening of the wind I felt that this unlucky gale would be the breaking point for a half-demoralised crew. Instead of getting somewhere we were fast losing ground to the south. By evening the wind had eased enough for us to let draw and start making north again towards Scoresby Sound. At least that was my proposal but the crew, the mate their spokesman, thought otherwise—demurred strongly and refused to do anything of the kind. Brian, of course, was as keen as I was to persevere but felt that his inexperience and his position as cook did not allow him an equal say. There we were in a stout ship, plenty of food and water, suffering a few inconveniences but certainly no hardships, and only some forty miles from our objective at just the right time of year.

Brian, John, and I argued, standing for some odd reason round the foot of the mast below. I knew it would be no use. I am not eloquent and it would have needed the fiery eloquence of a Drake or a Garibaldi to stiffen John's spine. Even the suggestion that if Scoresby Sound were ruled out we could go south to Angmagssalik, thus at least landing in Greenland, met with no favour. John reckoned that he had stretched himself to the limit for my sake, that he had reached the end of his tether, and that any delay might have serious effects upon his health. Cassandra Ken concurred and thought that if we were to go on, the chances of any of us even surviving were no better than fifty-fifty. Colin, with slightly less conviction, agreed. To give up when so near, in an able boat with ample supplies, was hard to stomach, but with an unwilling crew there was nothing to be done. 'Home, and don't spare the horses,' was the cry.

Once before I had had the melancholy experience of sailing homewards with a disillusioned crew. On this occasion the passage would be much shorter, so short that it should not be difficult to maintain harmony, to be polite instead of resentful. It proved not to be so short, and Brian did not feel it incumbent upon him to conceal his disgust at our ignominious flight and the man mainly responsible. For the first ten days we were almost as fogbound as we had been on the way out. For the sake of the record, not by way of complaint, I see from the logbook that between August 4th and 18th we had fog every day except on the critical 8th, when it rained. In the Greenland Sea fog is to be expected and like any other vexations and hazards of the sea must be borne with what cheerfulness one can muster. Like the ice conditions, fog may vary in intensity from year to year. On the Jan Mayen voyage of the previous year we had not nearly so much fog. We had struck a bad year, and the same had apparently held good, contrary to my belief, for the ice conditions. A friend in the Meteorological Office sent me this report:

> Our sea-ice charts for August and early September show that ice con-ditions for most of the time were excessive in the Scoresby Sound area. For the period 1st to 8th August open pack at the entrance and to seaward quickly became close pack within the Sound. Belts of close pack, 20 to 30 miles wide, existed to the north and south of the entrance and during the period 9th to 18th August, these belts merged, filled the entrance and combined with the close pack already within the Sound. The area of close pack extended 40 miles seaward of the entrance but a 10 to 20 miles wide bank of open pack lay along the coast to the south of Cape Brewster. The close pack gradually melted, more slowly within the Sound than outside, and by Septem-ber 7th open water existed over the whole area, though a belt of close pack lay just to the northward. After September 7th open and close pack continuously threatened and sometimes closed the entrance to the Sound.
>
> Thus the 'season' for Scoresby Sound was a very short one. *Sea Breeze* may well have been unable to make much progress into the Sound until late August and would have had considerable difficulty in clearing the entrance after the first week in September.

So much for the reports, but I have also an eye-witness account of con-ditions. Captain Toft was there again in *Ole Roemer*, met as much fog as we did, and concludes his letter with an interesting remark about the moral effects of fog and ice.

> We left Thorshavn July 30th and arrived at Scoresby Sound August 2nd. For most of the way we had dense fog with SE winds, but about 30 miles from the Greenland coast the fog disappeared and we got

clear weather. Very nice, but we then sighted a big area of heavy ice. Fortunately between the ice and Cape Brewster it was possible to force the ship through. It was very difficult and quite impossible for a vessel without ice protection and very strongly built. We tried to go to the roads (anchorage?) of Scoresby Sound but it was impossible owing to heavy ice.

We stayed in the area of Scoresby Sound until August 28th and from the first to the last day we had trouble with ice, sometimes being jammed in and drifting with it. The weather was bad, a rotation of three days of fog and snow, so it was an exceptionally bad season.

When we left we had difficulties with ice for the first eight miles. The weather was good until past Langanes when we had gale Force 9 for 36 hours. We arrived at Thorshavn August 31st after what I call a bad season.

After my experience, the best way to enter the Sound is from south-east close to Cape Brewster, but sailing along the east coast of Greenland will always be a little hazardous but quite interesting. Another problem is the crew. Not every man is fit for that job. I think that fog and ice is depressing for a young man.

At the time, from the little I had seen of the ice, I had thought that our chances were good. It is obvious from these reports that this was not so and that even with a less fainthearted crew, though we might have got into the Sound we could have done nothing, and might not have got out. Still that is no reason for not having tried.

CHAPTER IX

HOMEWARD BOUND

Fog alone was not responsible for our slow progress, but the light winds and calms that generally go with it. It is, however, possible to have the worst of both worlds and to enjoy fog and a gale at the same time, or even fog and a thunderstorm. Almost at the start of his historic voyage Slocum records:

> About midnight the fog shut down again denser than ever before. One could almost stand on it. It continued so for a number of days, the wind increasing to a gale. The waves rose high but I had a good ship. Still, in the dismal fog I felt myself drifting into loneliness, an insect on a straw in the midst of the elements. I lashed the helm, and my vessel held her course, and while she sailed I slept.

Lecky records a severe electric storm in the North Atlantic, the lightning forming a complete network of flashes, while the prevailing fog was so dense that the funnels could not be seen from the bridge.

Now that we were running away from Greenland we had nothing to fear from ice and therefore no necessity to heave to at night, or at least during the murkiest hours around midnight, as we had been doing. Bergs and floes generally show up whiter than the surrounding fog far enough away, say 200 or at the worst 100 yards, for a slow moving boat such as *Sea Breeze* to steer clear or stop. The ugliest menace is from bergy bits or small floes nearly awash that may not be seen at all, especially if the sea is a little rough; and there are the exceptional big bergs and floes that for some reason are an off-white colour or worse and blend perfectly with the surrounding fog. When such a berg does at last loom up and disclose itself it is likely to be close enough to frighten the helmsman out of his wits.

Ships were an unlikely hazard in fog in these waters. We did hear one ship hooting away as she crossed our bows some way off, near enough, however, to agitate John. With nautical punctilio he blew away on our squeaker fog-horn two blasts every minute, indicating, at any rate to the fulmars sitting on the water nearby, that we were a sailing vessel on the port tack. It would be valuable to know how far one of these lung-driven fog-horns carries, and on some calm, foggy day I must row off in the dinghy (with a compass!) to find out. One might not have far to row. Soon after this fog-horn contest, we observed another mystery of the sea that baffled even conjecture. We passed an open box measuring about six feet by two feet carrying at one end a short ensign staff flying a small flag with a St Andrew's cross. Had the box had a lid like a coffin one might have taken it for the funeral ship of some latter-day Viking of modest means launched on the ocean on its last voyage to Valhalla.

Head winds pushed us so far to the west that we had trouble in clearing Iceland and when the fog lifted we saw again the high land west of Langanes Peninsula. At last on the 20th we had all the wind we wanted. In one two-hour watch we did fourteen miles and made a day's run of 140 miles, urged on by big, following seas. We were on the wrong tack and I reckoned there was too much wind to gybe safely, so after supper—curry and macaroni cheese—we dropped the jib, brought her up into the wind, and round she went. Next day we went almost as fast, passed a Russian trawler and a factory ship, and sighted St Kilda well away to the northeast. There is little or no darkness in northern waters in June or July, only on the way home in late August or September is there any chance of seeing auroral displays, and since the night must also be cloudless, the opportunities are rare. The night after passing St Kilda we witnessed such a display, beginning with shafts of light like the beams of some colossal searchlight that soon dissolved to form a luminous band whose arch spanned the northern sky.

We made our landfall in the customary thick weather on August 23rd. Making a landfall infers some preciseness; it would be more correct to say that we inadvertently found ourselves close to a confusion of islands and islets at the southern end of the Hebrides. The wind being light and southerly I was tempted to make a fair wind of it by running off to the east through one of several unidentifiable sounds— Pabbay, perhaps, or Mingulay. I was not certain about any of them. Prudence, therefore, prevailed and we held on down the coast until we sighted the lighthouse on Berneray and knew exactly where we were. Off Barra Head we met plenty of wind and set a course for Skerryvore. Brian celebrated our arrival in home waters with curry and an apricot duff assuaged by white sauce.

After a windy night the day broke with vicious squalls hurrying down upon us from the north-west across a white-capped sea. What followed was probably my fault for not telling the helmsman, John, to steer wide, keeping the following wind well out on the quarter. Running fast before wind and sea with the whole mainsail set, the boat yawed quite a bit. The sight of a particularly threatening squall coming up astern, whipping the water white, decided me that it was time to reef. While down below getting into oilskins I felt the boat gybe and got back on deck to find the gaff dangling in two halves astride the topping lift, John having executed an imperial Chinese gybe. Taming the flogging mainsail and the flailing pieces of jagged wood took time and caution. That done, we set the topsail as a sort of trysail. Not a word of regret came from John who seemed to think that gaffs should be made of sterner stuff. Rathlin Island was already in sight and even under our diminished rig we went fast enough. The brave west wind carried us through the North Channel in style, enabling us to laugh at the adverse tide, a tide that on every previous passage had obliged us to anchor somewhere in order to escape it. Near Mew Island off Belfast Lough the wind began to take off.

Except in the unlikely event of carrying a fair wind all the way to Lymington, our trysail rig would prove a handicap and possibly a danger. Without a mainsail, for instance, we would not be able to claw off a lee shore, and the very next day we found ourselves in just those circumstances. We therefore decided to make for Holyhead to have the gaff repaired, and having gone there it would be only kind to look in at Barmouth to astonish the natives with a sight of *Sea Breeze.* That night the wind went south so that by morning we were off the Isle of Man coast south of Peel instead of south of the Calf of Man as we had hoped. The difficulty of sailing without a mainsail now became apparent. We were close to the shore, the wind blowing on to it, and whichever tack we tried, to the north-west or to the south-west, we could not get away from it. As we sagged to leeward towards an inhospitable bit of rugged coast I had the anchor got ready and told Ken to start the engine. The next ten anxious minutes passed slowly. Both fuel tanks were blocked and Ken was hastily rigging a jerrycan from which to feed fuel to the engine.

As we made down the coast with one perilous incident safely averted, I voluntarily incurred another. Wishing to cut short the pains of motoring I chose to take the passage through Calf Sound instead of going round outside the Calf of Man and Chicken Rock. If one stuck to mid-channel there were no dangers, though the Pilot did warn that the tide ran strongly and that the passage should not be attempted without local knowledge. I must say, when we came up to the pass and, when it was too late to turn back, saw the line of breaking water extending right across the extremely narrow opening, I began to have doubts about the wisdom of taking short cuts. Cassandra Ken had already given us up for lost. But all went well and on the east side of the island we soon picked up a wind. My mentor Lecky severely admonishes the mariner who tries short-cuts, and instances a 'major marine disaster that had recently occurred due to a fine ship being navigated at night through a narrow channel between a group of small islands and the mainland—all for the sake of a saving of five miles in distance steamed, during a round voyage (never completed) of some 12,000 miles.'

More recent experience confirms a suspicion that listening to the Shipping Forecasts is seldom of value. Out in the Atlantic beyond their range one forgets about forecasts and takes the weather as it comes, with no sense of any lost benefit; but in home waters listening becomes a habit that is not easily broken. There is always the chance of hearing something to one's advantage—a probable shift of wind, for instance, that might help to decide a course of action—and if not no harm is done. At six o'clock that evening, when halfway to Holyhead, we were surprised and a little disconcerted—for it might be right—to hear a gale warning for the Irish Sea. We expected to reach Holyhead by midnight but did not relish being caught in a westerly gale while searching for the entrance. On the other hand if we were to heave to to await the worst, we must do so forthwith while we still had ample searoom. The sky at sunset did not look strikingly ill-omened so we decided to stand on. The wind did increase to force 6—no more—but thanks to being set down by a strong tide we did not pass the Holy-head breakwater until well after midnight. Entering a strange port at night is not an exercise I enjoy and that night Holyhead seemed more than ordinarily confusing owing to the construction of a new breakwater then in progress and the presence of a floating crane with its web of mooring wires. We got in the way of the mail boat and in the end anchored too near the crane.

The Customs, who came on board early, treated us leniently, as they generally do if the case allows, and then piloted us to the boatyard where we landed the broken gaff. There was not enough water to stay there so we anchored off among a fleet of yachts. The boatyard had evidently suffered from some yachtsmen who 'payed with the mainsheet' as Slocum expresses it. Their first question was how I would pay them and through what bank? Three days elapsed before we could sail owing to the time needed for the proper hardening of the glued scarph. The gaff being ready, we bent on the mainsail and sailed out at mid-day of the 30th. More trouble with the fuel system had left us temporarily without the engine. In a light and fluky wind the tide carried us close to the North Stack which we narrowly avoided hitting thanks to a timely puff of wind and a hasty gybe. On so fine and warm a day, idling off the Anglesey coast was time well spent except that we wanted to catch the tide at Barmouth next day. There is a bar across the entrance that with our draught must be crossed within an hour or so of high water.

By midnight we were off Bardsey Island with a brisker wind and set a course for the Causeway Buoy that marks the seaward end of Sarn Badrig or St Patrick's Causeway, a dangerous rock ledge stretching from the shore for eleven miles out into Cardigan Bay. In the brief but glorious days of the Welsh trading schooners plying into the ports of Aberdovey, Barmouth, and Portmadoc, the Causeway claimed many victims. It is a natural causeway but runs so straight that it is easy to believe it to be the work of man, one of the embankments of the legendary kingdom of Cantref-y-Gwaleod, the 'Lowland Hundred', now sunk beneath the waters of Cardigan Bay. Readers of Peacock may remember the immortal Seithenym, a mighty toper, guardian of the embankment and answerable to the king for its safety, by whose drunken neglect it fell into decay. In the storm that one day breached the embankment, sweeping away all who were on it and engulfing the kingdom, Seithenym, instead of being drowned like the rest as he deserved, got safely ashore on one of the hundreds of wine barrels to which he had devoted his life industriously emptying.

We neither saw nor heard the Causeway Buoy, having evidently given it so safe a berth by keeping well south, that at ten o'clock next morning we fetched up near the Sarn-y-Bwch Buoy just south of Barmouth. From the sea the familiar long, flat ridge of Cader Idris that I have been looking at for the last twenty years appeared like a sharp peak, but Diffwys, a 2900-foot hill behind Bodowen, was unmistakable. Disregarding John's objections that we were off Portmadoc, we sailed up to the Outer Buoy where we jilled about waiting for high water. On *Mischief*'s one and only visit to Barmouth we had disappointed an official welcoming party by arriving twelve hours late, but on this gloriously fine Bank Holiday week-end people were too busy amusing themselves to bother about *Sea Breeze*. However, we were presently boarded by the harbour-master accompanied by an old friend of mine, Bob Henry, coastguard and Town Councillor, than whom there is no cheerier company. The Holyhead Customs, as I said, had treated us leniently, so we sat on deck watching the dinghy sailors and the bathing belles on the distant beach while the tide slowly rose and the level of the gin bottle swiftly fell. The wind had fallen away to nothing, so, assisted by our now inspirited guests, we handed the sails and motored in to lie at the small stone quay, the harbour-master imperiously shooing away a lobster boat to make room for us. After the boat had settled on the bottom and we had made sure she would not fall over we adjourned in relays for baths and food at Bodowen.

Next day we sailed with a gradually freshening northeasterly wind, made our departure from the Sarn-y-Bwch Buoy, and saw nothing more, except the Fishguard-Rosslare ferry, until Land's End loomed dimly out of the haze on the evening of September 3rd. Good going for 180 miles, and for me, good navigation. The Fishguard-Rosslare ferry, unlikely to be off course, gave us our latitude, and a combined sun and moon shot on the morning of the 3rd a fairly good fix. The mistakes one makes, when one is all adrift and off target by twenty or thirty miles, are seldom forgotten, so that it is heartening to record a bull's-eye.

Off Land's End the wind left us, apparently for good. Three days later we had struggled as far as the Start, some eighty miles on our way, and a laconic diary entry for that day reads: 'What a passage! Omelette and prunes.' Two days later in the same dull, thick, windless weather we were somewhere south-east of Portland Bill and making little progress. Having decided to motor the rest of the way we began a frantic search for a tin of engine oil that Ken reported the engine could not do without. No joy. (Emptying the ship at Lymington the tin was found lodged behind a frame in the stern locker.) Ken reckoned we could motor safely as far as Weymouth which we had already passed so back we went. Even that was not our last stop. Having missed the tide we anchored for the night in Swanage Bay to reach Lymington on the morning of the 9th.

Although *Sea Breeze* had taken us safely to the coast of East Greenland and back we had landed nowhere and achieved nothing. From that point of view the voyage could hardly be reckoned a success. On the other hand, if regarded as a trial run in a boat new to me, a shakedown cruise, it had won several prizes by the shaking down of no less than three spars. Despite that, and the leaking deck, I was happy with the boat and given time, which in my case is getting short, I shall become as fond of her as of *Mischief*.

The crew had scarcely come up to expectations. When they had assembled in June they had struck me as a most promising lot. Alas. As the hapless Duncan remarked:

> There's no art
> To find the mind's construction in the face:

and were there any such art I had at that time no alternative candidates upon whom it might have been exercised. At Appledore I had been lucky, and being then willing to take anyone at all to make up our numbers I had no reason to be dissatisfied. Three days later, *Sea Breeze* having been stripped to a gantline, the crew went their several ways. Looking at the old boat before I, too, started for home, I reflected that in the course of her long life she must have carried even rummer crews—skippers, too, for that matter; men who, unlike the boat herself, were not built to withstand the stress of sea and weather. Ships are all right, it's the men in them.

PART THREE

---◆---

Second Voyage in *Sea Breeze*

Summer 1970

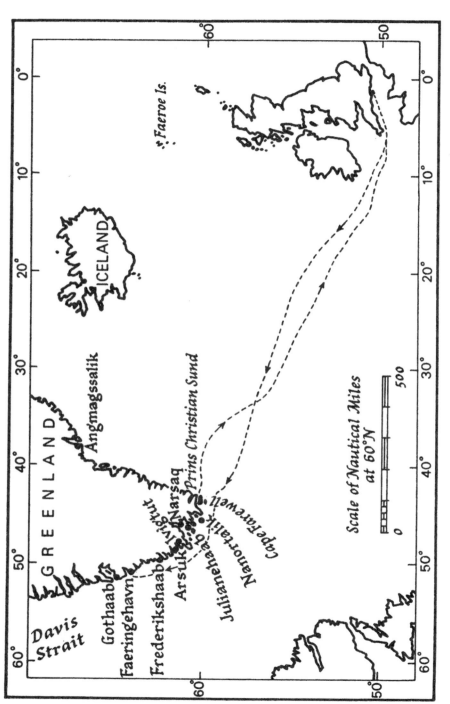

Map 4: To West Greenland

CHAPTER X

A DIFFERENT CREW

THREE MONTHS WENT BY while I pondered over the vicissitudes of life's voyage and voyages in general. In November of 1969 I had not even begun to think of crews or of where to go in 1970, nor had I had any of the usual enquiries. In fact since the loss of *Mischief* the assumption among those who made such enquiries may have been that I, too, had sunk or, at any rate, was fast sinking. After three successive setbacks one needed to be resilient—the troublesome voyage south of 1966–67, the disastrous voyage north of 1968 when through bad seamanship and worse luck I had lost faithful *Mischief*, and then the first futile voyage in *Sea Breeze*. But hope springs eternal even in my breast and to nourish it there came, like a ray of winter sunshine, a letter from Colin Putt whom I had not heard from since we had sailed together in *Patanela* in the winter of 1964–65 from Sydney to Heard Island.

His letter read:

David Lewis tells me that *Sea Breeze* has turned out to be a basically good ship, but that there is some difficulty in getting suitable crews; it struck me that this last point, awkward though it must be, might present me with an opportunity. There is between three and four months leave due to me in the next year; it becomes available in April and I can no doubt scrape up a return fare to England. If you are going on a short voyage in 1970 is there any possibility of my getting a berth in *Sea Breeze*. I should warn you that in addition to my established vices of eating and talking too much, and compulsive fiddling with rigging and machinery, I would probably be too short of leave to be of much use for fitting out. My friend Iain Dillon has asked me to make a similar plea on his behalf. He is an Australian, mountaineer and student of the classics, and has done a year in the Tasmanian cray-fish schooners. He is definitely no piker and although only 22 is one of the old school and believes in discipline for himself as well as others. PS. What sort of engine has *Sea Breeze*? I might be able to start reading about it.

Colin was then in charge of an I.C.I. chemical works in Sydney and, as I had fully realised in *Patanela*, was a man of infinite resource and ability. Probably, as Monty would say, a good man to go into the jungle with, had we been going there. More to my point, he was a good man to have if one was cast away on a desert island, where he would build you a boat were there enough driftwood about, and an engine, too, given some old iron. He has in hand at the present moment the building of a boat which is to be called *Reconnaissance*; as Colin explains, quoting a trite military maxim, time spent in reconnaissance is never wasted. Besides his technical abilities he has had long experience of expeditions in the mountains of New Zealand and New Guinea, as well as on Heard Island; and while not likely to do anything rash or ill considered he would not easily give up anything he had set himself to do. Nor was that all. He would more than make up for my own taciturnity. As the life and soul of any party, his copious loquacity, embellished with wit, wisdom, and anecdote, would take the weak minds of any crew off the small inconveniences of life at sea, such as cold, wet bunks, or seasickness.

Iain Dillon was an unknown quantity whom I was more than ready to take on Colin's recommendation. The word 'piker' is not in my vocabulary, but it is expressive enough and I thought I knew what Colin meant. Perhaps the majority of the crew on the previous voyage might have been shortly described as pikers. Besides his year spent at sea crayfishing, he had evidently done a lot of climbing; apparently unable or unwilling to settle down and content to earn enough money to enable him to go on expeditions. If he was anything like the Australians and New Zealanders that comprised *Patanela*'s crew, who regarded the ship they served in and the expedition they were part of as their only responsibility, I should have little to worry about and everything to hope for. Thus with these two as a solid nucleus, sheet anchor and kedge, so to speak, it would not much matter what the rest of the crew—supposing them to be pikers—either thought or did.

I had great hopes of Brian Potter coming again as cook, for the chances of finding any one in that capacity half so good, or so useful on board in every way, were remarkably slight. He had offered to come on the previous voyage mainly in the hope and expectation of climbing a Greenland mountain and had not even set foot in the country. Apart from his usefulness to me I felt I owed him another chance. But owing to some congenital defect his right hand was slowly seizing up—a brother of his suffered in the same way. The surgeon who operated in December assured him that the hand would be right within a month. Spring came and Brian's hand was of less use than Captain Hook's iron claw. He could hold a hammer with difficulty and did not think he was capable of grappling, as it were, with the problems of cooking at sea on an unstable platform, or even of moving about safely, when a sudden lurch of the boat might call for an equally sudden, strong grip of something. In the end I had to reconcile myself to counting him out.

Thus there were still two berths to fill. A friend connected with the Sail Training Association kindly had a notice of the intended voyage inserted in their news bulletin *Sail*—now for reasons of economy defunct. The two training ships *Sir Winston Churchill* and *Malcolm Miller* have between them made some one hundred and fifty cruises, carrying some thirty youngsters each time. I half expected, therefore, to be submerged by a flood of eager applicants for a four-month voyage for which they would not pay a thing. Two replied, one of whom, on hearing from me, silently withdrew. I met the sole survivor, Bob Comlay, on board *Sea Breeze* on one of my infrequent winter visits. Inside the boat in winter is like being in a crypt or a cave, one of those dripping caves. Water, a film of condensation, covers and drips from the deckhead and the beams. I am always surprised not to find incipient stalactites and stalagmites growing up to meet each other. Presumably the woodwork lacks carbonate of lime, or perhaps these visits I make, when I sleep on board with the stove going non-stop for forty-eight hours, are enough to nip the budding stalactites. Not only do these visits momentarily dry the boat out but I like to think that *Sea Breeze* feels she is not forgotten.

When Bob Comlay came, Brian Potter was also on board taking measurements for a locker door and a plate rack he was making for me. In those dank surroundings Bob looked a little pale and woe-begone but he made a good first impression. Instead of flicking cigarette ash about he asked for something to put it in, and when I started fiddling with the pump strum-box in the well of the bilge he at once lent a hand

and seemed to enjoy having his arms blackened with oily bilge water. He was very young, waiting to go to a university the next October, and was also slightly built—not likely to break a rope by heaving on it. Nevertheless, liking the look of him, I decided to take him and never had the slightest reason to regret it. Besides the highlight of the cruise in Sir Winston Churchill he had long been familiar with boats, had a brother who was a naval diver, and a sister who had done far more sailing than he had. A sore point, but a Greenland cruise would put that family quarrel right. He therefore knew something about boats and, as I soon found, was never backward in making suggestions, a few of which, annoyingly enough, turned out to be right. He was extremely keen, put the boat first and foremost, did not forget his obligations to me, always asking for more work, and was generally first on deck and last to leave. In short the type of lad that one has a right to expect from those who offer to go on voyages of this kind.

I had yet to find a cook and since time was getting short played my last card, a card that before now had turned up trumps. I advertised in *The Times*, taking care to say that I wanted an amateur cook of the male species. It was a perfectly straightforward advertisement, no glamour or flat-catching bait, even stating where we were going, and it brought a dozen replies. Things and men are not what they used to be. A similar but much earlier advertisement had brought twice as many replies, though that may have been owing to the tantalising way in which it had been worded, giving nothing away: 'Hands wanted for long voyage in small boat. No pay, no prospects, not much pleasure.' Half the replies to that came from girls or women and I had to pay for my failure to be explicit by writing a great number of explanatory letters giving my reasons for not taking them.

In spite of the precise stipulations in the present case a few of those who did reply obviously expected to be paid for their services, and one confessed to being of the wrong sex. Georgina did not claim to be a cordon bleu as one or two of those earlier applicants had, nor did she say anything about her ability to arrange flowers, but she sounded the right sort, 'devoted to slave labour and amateur cooking'. She said not a word about sea experience or even the sea, so perhaps she had never seen it. But neither had Brian Potter for that matter, except from the deck of a steamer. I was sorely tempted to take Georgina at her word until I considered what effect the springing of such an unlikely and possibly unwelcome surprise might have on Colin and Iain. Would Colin's conversational flow have to be muted or even stopped? Was Iain accustomed to mixed bathing?

From the twelve possibles I had little difficulty in choosing. After eliminating the professionals out of hand, Georgina with reluctance, and one or two others who sounded odd, the remaining six, all but one, eliminated themselves. When I met him, though I did not tell him so, Andrew Harwich was the only candidate. He lived in London, as so many people do, and playing for safety I arranged to meet him at the Royal Geographical Society. I remembered that on one or two occasions I had foolishly arranged to meet an unknown candidate at a suitably square club that I occasionally haunt, and the consequent embarrassment caused by my having to borrow a tie from the hall-porter before my man was eligible to enter. Besides their own far-flung Fellows, the Royal Geographical Society give house room to the Everest Foundation and the Institute of Navigation, so that they can ill afford to be stuffy about whom they allow to pass their doors—perhaps, they are not stuffy enough. Their hall-porter must be well accustomed to admitting some queer fish, foreigners and such like.

When a youth with hair down to his shoulders walked in I knew, or rather feared, that this was the chap, for I had noticed him walking up and down in pensive fashion just before the appointed hour. If Andrew was equally taken aback by my appearance he managed to conceal it, as I hope I did my own misgivings. Like Bob he was young and also waiting to go to a university, as it happened St Andrews with which I have a suitably vague and tenuous connection. He could not be expected to have had any experience of the sea or of expeditions but he said he could cook and enjoyed cooking, which is half the battle. At this stage not wishing to discourage him, I did not tell him I had seen Colin eating, and that probably Iain, that much younger, was not likely to be left at the post in the table stakes. Andrew was then passing his time and earning pocket-money by working in a garage as a petrol-pump attendant, an experience that might come in useful to us though at the moment I could not see when. At this interview he may have been over-awed by the picture of some famous explorer leering down at him, Stanley perhaps, or Doughty. He did not say much, I am not fluent, and in a short time he was due back at his petrol pump. For the sound reason that I had no one else in view I agreed to take him and he agreed to come, and I could not have made a wiser decision. His long hair, apart from getting in the way, did not unfit him for life at sea. Without any break Andrew cooked every meal, and cooked them well, from start to finish. Curries and duffs, which in my view more deserve the name of 'sea-food' than lobsters, crabs, and such like, flowed from the galley in agreeable abundance. By the time we were homeward bound, appetites having grown by eating, the duffs had to be cooked in a bucket. Besides this Andrew took an afternoon watch and allowed neither gales, fog, nor ice to perturb him. If Colin, the New Zealander, and Iain, the Australian, set an extremely high standard, my two young Englishmen were not far behind.

In 1968 we had been in the same latitude and within 300 miles of Scoresby Sound, and in 1969 we had sighted the cape to the south of it. Before the news of Colin's advent I had naturally intended having a third go. But in any one season the chances of success are sketchy and it would not do to court another failure with Colin and Iain on board. They were coming to climb, coming a long way, and I could not afford to disappoint their hopes in that respect as might well happen. Even if we were successful we were hardly likely to be inside the Sound before the middle of August, allowing us a bare fortnight ashore before having to start for home. Reluctantly therefore I abandoned the Scoresby Sound plan, the more reluctantly because I looked like having the sort of crew that would succeed were success at all possible.

I decided instead to try South-west Greenland, Julianehaab and fjords to the south, where there are plenty of mountains of the order of 5000 to 7000 feet, and where I myself had not been before. Owing to badly under-estimating the severity of the ice conditions this proved to be a mistake in that we had too little climbing. On the other hand we had a voyage full of incident and gained a great deal of ice experience. I was aware that we would meet ice off that coast but did not imagine that it would make us nearly a month late in reaching our chosen fjords.

Ice conditions off the west coast of Greenland are peculiar. In early summer north of Upernivik in Lat. 72° N there will be ice near the coast, part of the Baffin Bay ice which is known as the Middle Pack. From there southwards to about Lat. 63° N, around Fiskernaesset,

Colin filling a jerrycan with fresh melt-water

Fast in the pack

there is unlikely to be any ice other than icebergs; while south of that again, right down to Cape Farewell, there will be heavy pack-ice. This is what the Danes call the 'Storis' or Large Ice, massive floes two or three years old originating in the polar basin and carried down the east coast of Greenland by the East Greenland current. By early spring the 'Storis' will have reached Cape Farewell and begins to extend west and north-west as a belt of ice anything from twenty to thirty miles wide following the trend of the coast. By April it will have filled the Juliane-haab Bight and spread further up the coast to as far as Fiskenaesset or even Faeringehavn some 350 miles from Cape Farewell.

On its journey from Cape Farewell it becomes less dense owing to the comparatively warmer water of Davis Strait, and with the advance of summer it begins to disintegrate, more quickly towards its north-ern limit. By the end of June in a normal year, though the Julianehaab Bight will still be choked with ice, north of that the ice will be widely scattered. Thus a small vessel bound for Julianehaab would hope to be able to reach the coast to the north of the Bight early in July and then by means of fjords and the open water generally found inside the sker-ries that fringe the coast, work her way back to Julianehaab or any of the fjords to the south.

Obviously then, in order to reach the coast early in the summer and to enjoy a full climbing season the place to go is between Lat. 63° N and Lat. 70° N where one would meet no pack-ice at all. *Mis-chief*'s first and second voyage to Greenland had been to that region and it was on that account less attractive to me for 1970; and if it had been a 'normal' ice season the plan we had chosen would have worked out pretty well.

The fjords at the back of the Julianehaab Bight—the worst place on the west coast for ice—are those where the Vikings had their princi-pal settlement, the Osterbygd or Eastern settlement. Having seen the quantity of ice off this coast, the first question that occurs to one is how the Vikings had managed. They were undoubtedly bold and skilful seamen but surely, one thought, even the boldest and most land-hun-gry Viking would have thought twice before choosing to settle upon such an ice-strewn coast. The accepted explanation is that the climate was then warmer and that there was in fact no ice. Professor Gwyn Jones in *The Norse Atlantic Saga* has this to say:

There is a wealth of evidence of various kinds which allows modern scientists to conclude that during the climatic optimum of A.D. 1000 to 1200 the mean summer temperatures in southern Greenland were 2°C. to 4°C. higher than now and that sea temperatures in the northernmost Atlantic were of the same order of increase. The area of permanent ice lay north of 80°N., drift-ice must have been rare south of 70°, and very rare indeed south of the Arctic Circle. There is therefore no reason rooted in climate for disbelieving the Norse voyages to Greenland and the mainland of North America.

But in terms of the Greenland settlement the important thing to establish is not that the climatic optimism was warmer than our own warm period but that it was succeeded by a period decidedly, and in the event, fatally colder. Here, too, literary, historical, archaeological, meteorological, and climatic evidence leads to the same conclusion; that after A.D. 1200 the climate of the northern hemisphere fell progressively for two hundred years or more and that by c. 1430 Europe had entered a little Ice Age. Over much of Europe the glaciers were beginning to advance, the tree line fell lower, vegetation and harvests were diminished by the cold; and, worst of all for the Greenlanders, the sea temperature sank, causing an immense increase in the drift-ice which comes south with the East Greenland current.

In an article in the *Geographical Journal* Mr H. H. Lamb of the Meteorological Office, who is in charge of research on climatic variation, wrote as follows:

> There is no reasonable doubt that the Arctic was a bit warmer, and that there was less ice on the northern seas, when the old Norse voyages to Iceland and Greenland were made, especially between A.D. 1000 and 1200, than has been the case since. Ice was increasingly encountered on the old sailing route, which crossed to East Greenland near the Arctic Circle, from 1203 onwards; and by 1350–1400 this route had to be abandoned for one further south, rounding Cape Farewell. After 1410 there was no regular communication between Europe and any part of Greenland until the 1720s; the old Norse colony died out, and no European ship ever got in through the ice even on the south-west coast after 1605.

CHAPTER XI

TO CAPE FAREWELL

———————◆———————

S AILING DAY HAD PROVISIONALLY been fixed for June 5th. Colin could not arrive before the end of May and Iain not until June 2nd. I gathered he was earning money for the air fare by working in a West Australian mine. Since there were only three of us available for fitting-out, Bob, Andrew, and I lived on board from May 20th onwards. During the winter, if the boat could be got dry enough, I had begun brightening up inside by slapping white paint over the original pastel blue. Slapping is the word, for I was working against time. Bob, who lives at Portsmouth, managed to complete the job in time for us to make ourselves at home on board. Having renewed the ratlines and set up most of the running rigging we faced the problem of the boom, a very heavy spar that the combined strength of two striplings and a man weak with age could barely lift. It had to be got out of a shed, trundled over to the boat, and hoisted to its fitting on the mast. Like the pyramid-builders, but without their advantage of numbers, we had to use our brains, and by dint of a trolly and tackles succeeded admirably. Compared with the boom the weight of the bowsprit is trifling but it cannot be rove from inboard as there is not enough room on the foredeck. The stern of the boat has to be swung out and the bow brought in so that the bowsprit can be launched from the quayside butt-first through the gammon-iron.

With all that done and the boat fully rigged we had time in hand and set to work scraping the deck to the bare wood. At various times the deck had had several coats of paint of different colour and quality and there were numerous worn patches where water could get under the paint and remain so that some of the planks never dried. Some of the old paint could be peeled off with the fingers but there were places where it withstood the attack of the largest scraper we had, a two-handed weapon with a head like a three-sided battle-axe. The bare deck looked well enough when finished though I suspect this

treatment made the leaks worse, some of the pitch between the planks
having been disturbed by the scrapers.

Colin wasted no time in London. Having arrived at midday of the
29th, he joined us that evening, bowed down by a colossal rucksack
and clutching a correspondingly heavy ice-axe. The axe, like most of
his gear, was of his own making, designed to deal with adamantine
New Zealand ice, and modelled, one thought, on the axes with which
Swiss guides hewed their way up Mont Blanc early in the last century. His rucksack, and climbing gear such as windproof and gloves,
were all home-made, a little *outré*, perhaps, and lacking in finish, but
undeniably effective. If all of us were as proficient, many shops would
have to put up the shutters. Vehicles, of course, are well within Colin's
scope. I remember seeing at Sydney—indeed I must have ridden in
it—the 'Puttmobile', a hybrid monster, part truck, part motor car, part
mobile crane, reminding one of those Eskimo carvings known as 'tubi-
laks' that portray a mythical creature with the head of a musk-ox, the
body of a bird, and the feet of a bear.

Colin had sent by sea two large drums, one containing an armoury
of tools—spanners, chisels, saws, 7 lb. hammer, mallets, files, and a full-
size adze. All the chisels, by the way, were made from old files, and
were looked after, like the rest of the tools, with a craftsman's care,
wiped over daily when at sea with a secret mixture to keep rust at bay.
In the other drum were six gallons of Australian wine or 'plonk' and a
quantity of dried fruit. The wine in big glass jars had stood the journey
well and no more deserved the pejorative name of 'plonk' than most
of the red wine we drink in England. Within minutes of arriving Colin
had changed into working rig, opened up the tool drum, and begun
making tentative advances towards the engine.

Iain arrived as planned and instead of the lean-faced, hungry-look-
ing clean-shaven Australian I had expected, he wore a beard, and the
removal of this beard some months later revealed an almost chubby
face. More surprising still was his voice—quiet and rather more English than the English. So we were able to sail as planned on Friday
June 5th. Only a few Lymington friends watched us go—no one from
the yard who, perhaps, thought they would soon see us again as had
happened before. *Sea Breeze* may be regarded there as an anachronism
but she is useful as a sort of chopping-block upon which apprentices

can be let loose to try their unpractised hand, for since she is thick little harm can result. On a fine day with an easterly breeze we could not have wished for a better start. Outside the Needles the slight sea affected only Andrew who had so far recovered by the Sunday that we had our usual curry and a masterly duff, washed down with Australian Moselle. Off Anvil Point, of all unlikely places, we were pursued by a patrol boat and brusquely told to steer south as a missile was about to be fired. We ran down Channel at record speed until the Saturday night when, with the Wolf light in sight, the wind headed us. So we bore off to the south and next morning in fine, but hazy weather rounded the Bishop Rock and set off westwards.

Colin apparently disliked carrying birds as passengers. When a racing pigeon settled down to roost on the masthead, out of harm's way and harming no one, he lashed a broom to the burgee halyards and promptly dislodged it. Besides pigeons we had some minor worries. The log, which had recently been overhauled, revolved only by fits and starts. Until the spinning rotator had wound the line into kinks, the register mechanism refused to budge when it would suddenly let go spinning madly and stopping again as soon as the line had unwound. No line could stand that sort of treatment for long and in a few days the line broke and we lost the rotator. It was not much missed. With a little experience the man on watch can estimate within a mile or so how many miles he has done in the watch. Bob made a Dutchman's log which we used occasionally, or we would throw a chip of wood over at the stem and time its passage for the length of the boat. If Andrew was handy he would give you the speed in knots before you had time to write anything down. My sextant had likewise been overhauled with the result that when taking a sight I found I had three suns to choose from, a bright sun in the middle with lesser luminaries above and below. A little confusing at first, but so long as one stuck to the same sun the sights worked out all right.

After sighting the Fastnet light we ran out of wind and into fog, hearing in due course the explosive fog signals from Mizzen Head and later the bellowing of the Bull lighthouse. There is a perfect menagerie of names in that region—Bull island with its neighbouring islets of Cow, Calf, and Heifer, not to mention the Cat and Crow rocks. Winds remained light and progress slow in spite of having everything set including the genoa. Try as we might the wind could not be persuaded to fill both headsails, there was not enough of it. I could sympathise with the good people of Steeple Bumpstead, Bucks., who are said to have refused to allow the building of a second windmill on the grounds that there was barely enough wind for the one they already had. Even after that rush down Channel the whole passage proved slow, so slow that the average daily run for the Atlantic crossing was only sixty-eight miles.

On the 16th, when we had some wind and a lot of rain, we did our best run of 130 miles. The rain, and the water that *Sea Breeze* scooped up as she heeled over, soon found a way below. We had to rig a sort of plastic aqueduct along the beams to canalise the drips, leading the water into a tin suspended at one end of the beam. No one seems to have thought of rigging a tin at both ends, so that if the boat were put on the other tack one had to remember to transfer the tin to the leeward side. The hydraulic pump started a leak, too, turning the galley floor into a skating rink. To put this right involved draining the whole system of oil which Colin managed to do without losing too much.

A few hundred miles west of Ireland put us beyond the range of the BBC Home Service and in order to get time signals we listened occasionally to the Overseas Service, and, having got the time signal, usually switched off before the tale of world events began to unfold. At sea only the events within our small world bounded by the visible horizon were of much interest, the sighting of a ship, a school of dolphins, or a whale, having far more impact than wars and rumours of wars. We saw nothing of pronounced interest except on the night Bob called me up to look at a mysterious, luminous object astern which I had no difficulty in pronouncing to be the rising moon.

As I said, we seldom listened to the news, but quite by chance on June 19th, when we were still some 500 miles from Cape Farewell, we heard the result of the General Election. Our two 'colonials' took the news calmly but were happy to join me in what the cheerful Frenchmen that Colin and I had met at Kerguelen called a 'coup de whisky', while Andrew appropriately dished up bully in batter and Cabinet pudding. I see from my gastronomic diary that he had begun reaching out for higher if less filling things than duffs, such as chocolate soufflé and apricot pie. Besides wine we had our full ration of spirits, usually broached only once a week on Saturday night. Except on the homeward run, when with a large surplus on hand, on which duty would have to be paid, we set ourselves seriously to reducing it.

Although we met no full gales we were sometimes obliged to heave to. On one occasion in the early hours of the morning, when the crew were having trouble handing the jib preparatory to heaving to, I lashed the tiller and went forward to offer some unwanted advice. The boat came up into the wind and before I could unlash the tiller she went about with a violent lurch accompanied by a quite appalling crash from below. A big shelf carrying all our wine jars, sextant, binoculars, and spare Primus stoves had come bodily away. Only one jar had broken but obviously the rest would be the better if drunk quickly. Mummery and his guide Burgener, on the Furggen ridge of the Matterhorn, had reasoned similarly: 'Immediately in front, the long, pitiless slabs, ceaselessly swept by whizzing, shrieking fragments of all sorts and sizes, suggested to Burgener—who had a most prudent and proper objection to waste—that it would be well to drink our Bouvier before any less fitting fate should overtake it.'

Head winds rather than lack of wind accounted for our poor average mileage. For us the distance to Cape Farewell was about 1700 miles, a little less than the distance from north of Bergen in Norway whence the Vikings sailed in their long ships and apparently sailed faster; only seven days to Horn at the north-west corner of Iceland, and four more days to Greenland. Professor Gwyn Jones in *A History of the Vikings* quotes these 'sailing directions' culled from Icelandic sources—most concise directions, no need to be written, capable of being carried in the thickest Viking skull:

Learned men state that from Stad (north of Bergen) in Norway it is seven days sail west to Horn in the east of Iceland; and from Snaefellsness, where the distance is shortest, it is four days sail west to Greenland. And it is said if one sails from Bergen due west to Hvarf (a south-east Greenland landmark) that one's course will lie some seventy miles or more south of Iceland... One sails north of Shetland so that one sights land in clear weather only, then south of the Faeroes so that the sea looks halfway up the mountainsides, then south of Iceland so that one gets sight of birds and whales from there.

The Gokstad Viking ship, built about A.D. 850 and retrieved from a burial mound in 1880 looks a fast ship. In 1893 a replica of the Gokstad ship was sailed across the Atlantic from Bergen to Newfoundland in twenty-eight days. The original ship was seventy-six feet overall with a beam of seventeen feet, and she had a keel of fifty-seven feet made from a single oak timber—the similar piece of timber for the replica had to be imported from Canada. On the direct route north of Iceland there would certainly be a good chance of favourable easterly winds since most of the depressions would pass south of Iceland, but towards the end of the Viking period circa 1300 the worsening ice conditions had forced the abandonment of this route. It is thought, and it must be almost certain, that the big single squaresail slung on a yard some thirty-seven feet long on a mast some thirty-five feet high was fitted with a kind of sprit, making it like a lugsail, so that the boat could sail 'on the wind' as well as with a following wind.

Despite head winds, and the drips from which all our bunks suffered in some degree, the crew were in remarkably good spirits. Alone on watch in the cockpit, the rain perhaps pelting down, it did one good to hear the gales of laughter wafted up from below as the crew sat yarning after a meal while the sea-water used for washing up was heating. Iain had one of the heartiest laughs I have ever heard, a laugh easily aroused that far out-bellowed anything that wind or sea might be doing in that way. Well furnished with argument and exposition, Colin had, too, an endless fund of stories and anecdotes, mainly about the strange characters who still haunt the outback, as the Australians call their hinterland. He had read widely, having at one time, I think, been a teacher, and what is more difficult, remembered what he had read. Bob's studies were to be directed to electronics and computers, Andrew's to mathematics, so that they had something in common to expound—subject to correction by the omniscient Colin—and much to disagree about. Unlike with some of my past crews, no roster for the duty of galley-slave had to be kept. As a matter of course all lent a hand with the washing-up and the sweeping or washing down of the saloon. Colin hardly ever sat still. He was either busy at the work-bench making something—an oven, perhaps, or new chocks for the dinghy—or working on the engine. Among many other things he entirely reorganised the fuel system. During the winter the three tanks that had given us

Iain posing, after shaping a bollard with his ice-axe

Trying to take a sun-sight in a tin of oil on top of the compass housing

trouble on the previous voyage had been taken out and cleaned. Whoever put them back had omitted to chock them off properly, as we discovered when they began to move in the first rough weather we met.

On June 30th we were by account sixty miles south of Cape Farewell. For the last few days we had had to fight to gain any northing having early on been too intent on getting to the west. On a crossing to Greenland, when head winds are met, it generally pays to stay on the port tack thereby at least saving a little distance. At this stage we began reaping the first fruits of Colin's oven. Iain made currant buns for tea, eaten hot, and we were able to have our potatoes baked in their jackets. Food plays an important part at sea—all ills are good when attended by food—and I hope these frequent references to it may dispel a myth, current since Himalayan days, that to climb or sail with the writer spells slow starvation.

Icebergs are sometimes seen 100 miles from Cape Farewell and the Pilot recommends giving the cape a berth of seventy miles. We were surprised, therefore, next morning when I reckoned we were only some thirty miles to the south-west that no icebergs were in sight. When the sky cleared I got a noon sight and found that we were forty miles west-south-west of the cape and still no ice in sight. The afternoon turned out gloriously fine. Our first iceberg came in sight, the growling of pack-ice could be heard, and presently we made out the long line of ice stretching far to westward. By seven o'clock of a calm, sunny evening, the wind having fallen light, we lay to about a mile off the edge of the ice. The sea temperature had fallen to 33° F. Icebergs, however big, do not seem to affect the sea temperature in their vicinity, but in the proximity of a field of pack-ice the effect is very marked.

Thinking in all innocence that the crew might not have another such favourable chance of observing pack-ice at close quarters we sailed in close enough for them to take photographs. Often at the edge of the pack there is a wide region of scattered floes that tempts or obliges one to penetrate further in order to discover whether the main body of the pack is likely to be navigable. At this stage, of course, we had no such design and, had we had, could at once have laid it aside. On that bright evening, the sun still high in the sky, we lay to within a cable's length of a solid, glistening white wall of anything up to twenty feet in height. Such dense, closely packed ice I had never seen.

CHAPTER XII

IN THE ICE

W ITH JUST ENOUGH WIND TO SAIL we let draw and followed the ice-edge to the north-west. That night—it was, of course, light all night—an east-bound Norwegian whale-chaser closed us in order to exchange greetings. An Irish monk Dicuil, writing in the year 825, describes with accuracy the light northern nights of Iceland:

> The setting sun hides itself at the evening hour as if behind a little hill, so that no darkness occurs during that very brief period of time, but whatever task a man wishes to perform, even to picking the lice out of his shirt, he can manage it precisely as in broad daylight.

Incidentally, in what sort of craft did these Irish monks, who were neither trained seamen nor expert boat-builders like the Norsemen, reach Iceland a hundred or two hundred years before the latter?

For the next week, mostly in fog, drizzle, or heavy rain, we made up the coast, standing out to the west when headed, and then standing in again to keep in touch with the ice, always expecting, as we got further north, to find it becoming more open. We had no intention of trying to reach the coast until in the latitude of Nunarssuit, an island about 120 miles to the north-west of Cape Farewell. The island lies on the north side of Julianehaab Bight, separated from the mainland by Torsukatak Sound, the channel commonly used by trading vessels when coasting inside the skerries and by which Julianehaab can be reached by a sort of back-door entrance, thus avoiding the ice-filled Bight. The success of this plan much depended on our obtaining sights for latitude and whether ice would permit our getting close enough to the Torsukatak entrance to identify it. To make out the small beacon marking the entrance to the Sound we should have to be well within the three-mile limit.

After twenty-four hours of steady rain, the following day found us hove to in a short, steep sea raised by a stiff northwesterly breeze.

For what it was worth, and at the cost of a shower-bath, I managed to take a sight. When we let draw that evening we soon sighted ice a mile ahead, went about, and steered west. When we next closed with the ice we had a fair wind which allowed us to keep the ice in sight as we sailed to the north-west. We had had no sights for latitude but I assumed that by now we were well beyond Nunarssuit. Our hopes now centred on making Arsuk, a small port thirty miles further up the coast.

Close north-west of Torsukatak Sound there is a group of no less than 150 skerries, a feature, I had thought, by which the Sound would be far more readily identified than by any beacon. Early on the morning of July 5th the sight of a number of black objects convinced me that my reckoning was out and that we had most opportunely and by accident stumbled on these skerries. Calling Iain, I put the boat about and steered to pass round their western edge. On this drizzly morning, even from quite close, it took us a long time to decide that the black things were in fact icebergs, and the improving light left no room for doubt. Turning back to continue along the ice-edge, an edge that looked as dense and uncompromising as ever, I happened to glance astern and saw a large passenger ship of some 5000 tons with a tripod mast, slowly emerge from the ice about two miles away. Outside the ice she stopped and lay to. I expected her presently to steam north-west in our direction. But she remained stationary and before I could make up my mind to go back, fog came down. Thus we missed a chance of speaking to her and at least finding out where we were. We learnt later that she was the monthly passenger ship on the Copenhagen-Greenland run trying without success to reach Arsuk and Ivigtut.

For most of the day we held on north-west through widely scattered floes, gybed once to escape from a cul-de-sac, and towards evening were again forced out to the west. After losing the little we had gained towards the east, and still surrounded by scattered floes, we hove to for the night. Curry and duff as usual, for it was Sunday night. Since our near encounter with the ship we had seen no heavy ice. I began to hope that the scattered floes we were among marked the northernmost drift of the Storis and that even if we could not fetch Arsuk, then Frederikshaab, the next port up the coast, would be easily attainable. As we learnt later, Frederikshaab was at this time closed to all shipping by ice. Fog held us up next morning until noon when a wan sun and a vague horizon allowed me to take a sight for latitude. It put us in Lat. 61° 30′ N., halfway between Arsuk and Frederikshaab, which was probably correct. We gained some more miles towards the land through gradually lessening ice until dense fog obliged us once more to stop. With the air temperature 35° F. and the sea only 31° we needed a lot of clothes.

'A long and trying day' is how my diary describes July 7th. In a small, unstrengthened vessel it is mere prudence not to enter close pack unless one knows that there is open water beyond and how far beyond. If the floes increase and the open water between them becomes less it is folly to persevere and common sense to turn back. These solemn truths were not learnt that day, they were merely heavily underlined. I knew them before, and for that reason the anxious hours that now followed were the more galling. In a flat calm we started motoring north-east through open pack that soon threatened to become worse. Instead of turning back we headed more to the north on the facile assumption that we were near the northern limit of the drift. In a short time there was no longer a question of steering a course, we had to take whatever lead offered, and many of these so-called leads led to nothing but trouble. When we got stuck, which was far too often, it might take a quarter of an hour or more to free ourselves. With her small, offset propeller, *Sea Breeze* needs a lot of room in which to turn. For manoeuvring in ice one wants a boat that will spin round in her own length.

Bob and Iain spent the day in turns high up the shrouds conning the boat, spying out the leads, and looking for signs of open water. They could not see far, visibility being about 300 yards. As the day wore on I had uneasy visions of spending the night and even being crushed in this icy wilderness, cheek by jowl with some of the ugliest ice I had seen, jagged, misshapen, old polar floes ten to twenty feet high, and, what was worse, always on the move, the leads closing and opening with bewildering speed. Like men in a maze, lost to all sense of time and direction, we sought only to escape. Having probed in various directions, we now ignored all leads except those that trended south, the way by which we had entered our maze, and at last towards evening, to our great joy, the ice began to relent and we reached a large polynia (space of open water surrounded by ice). There we hove to while we supped appropriately off pasta and prunes. The fog then lifted and we sighted land a long way off. Much heartened we pushed on through fairly open water until at 1 a.m. we stopped for cocoa and rum and some much needed rest. When hove to, even in the largest polynias, there were always some floes about; the man on watch had to watch our drift, and on drawing near to a floe had to judge whether we would drift safely by or whether he must let draw and sail clear.

Andrew took my watch and I turned in thankful to have won clear and pretty certain that I knew where we were. During that brief glimpse of the land I was sure I had seen the Frederikshaab glacier away to the north-east. I had seen it before on an earlier voyage from well out to sea, and it is the only glacier on this part of the coast. This ten-mile wide glacier flowing down from the ice-cap some thirty-five miles beyond Frederikshaab makes an unmistakable landmark. No bergs can calve from this glacier for it ends on a flat which dries. The glacier showed up clearly enough in the morning when we hoisted sail and set off hopefully to the south-east in the direction of Frederikshaab. As the floes increased again we resorted to the engine. For sailing, the floes must be pretty wide apart, five-tenths ice cover at the most. Given room and a fair wind the floes can be dodged easily enough under sail, but if the wind is fresh the boat may be going too fast to stop in time should a mistake have been made and a collision appear imminent. For that reason fore and aft rig is less handy than a squaresail which when backed stops the boat short. A few Victorian yachtsmen who were rich enough to have large paid crews had a liking for northern waters. One of them, Leigh Smith, who has a Spitsbergen cape named after him, eventually lost his yacht *Eira* in the ice off Franz Josef Land in 1881. Another, James Lamont, whose hobby was killing walrus, used to sail his 142-ton schooner to Spitzbergen and then transfer to a much handier thirty-ton sloop with a squaresail, having discovered that his fore-and-aft schooner was unsuited to ice navigation.

When the engine had to be stopped for a minor repair we tried the experiment of mooring to a floe in order to stop the boat drifting, the wind being very fresh. Selecting a good big floe with a clean-cut edge and no projecting tongues—nothing like those craggy miniature icebergs of the previous day — ideally with a little indented bay like a small dock, we would put our stem gently against the ice while two of the crew jumped from the bowsprit with ice-axes and mooring ropes.

The floe needed to have some hummocks that with ice-axes we could quickly fashion into bollards, for in an otherwise well-found ship we lacked ice-anchors. That our first floe had not been well chosen we realised when a large piece broke off. We moored to another where we decided to stay for a while, the wind having freshened to a good force 6, and blowing, of course, straight from Frederikshaab. We were low on fuel and could not afford to waste any by punching into a strong head wind. With so much ice still about we realised that we depended largely on our engine.

The floe to which we moored, as well as all the ice in the vicinity, was constantly in motion. Consequently we soon found ourselves hemmed in. At midnight we managed to escape and moored to yet another floe. Twice more we repeated the performance until on the afternoon of the 9th, when we felt we were secure for some time, attached as we were to a really well chosen floe with a mile or more of open water to leeward. Not a bit of it. Within an hour ice began streaming into the polynia and this time we were not smart enough in casting off surrounded by several miles of tight-packed floes of all shapes and sizes intermingled with some vast icebergs. The floe we had picked on was a beauty, nearly 100 yards in length, the one half flat as a lawn, and on the side we were moored amply provided with hummocks that afforded bollards for head-ropes, stern-ropes, breast-ropes, springs, the lot. They came in mighty handy when we had to warp the boat forward or back to avoid some threatening neighbour. Through pressure and rafting these old polar floes are thick, unlike the sea-ice that results from one winter's freeze, which would not be more than five feet thick—the sort of ice in which the old whalers and sealers were able with ice-saws to cut themselves a safe dock. In the clear water one could follow the emerald green face of our floe down for twenty feet and there would probably be as much again below that.

During the five days of our imprisonment we kept normal watches except when at night, if the ice was restless, we kept double watches. The two men might well find themselves sweating while they fended off floes with our spiked poles or trudged about on the ice shifting mooring lines. On first realising that we were well and truly beset Colin had suggested having some survival gear ready on deck or on the floe in case the boat got nipped and we had to abandon her. We

Moored to a floe in a polynia

would, I thought, have good warning when any pressure started, and I
doubt if we ever were in danger of being nipped, the few yards of open
water that generally surrounded our floe affording that much 'give'.
Nor was there ever any tossing about of the ice which would soon have
knocked holes in *Sea Breeze*, for the many miles of ice that lay between
us and the open sea perfectly damped any swell or motion. We lay as
quiet as in a dock. Nevertheless we were by no means free from anxiety,
especially at first before we had become inured and reconciled to our
strange position. Even with several northern voyages behind me I had
no experience of this sort of thing. Perhaps I had had more sense then.
In Baffin Bay, in Lancaster Sound, off Baffin Island, or on the east coast
of Greenland, we had seldom become entangled with ice and never for
long. On the east coast of Greenland we had once been in heavy pack
and had suffered for it, but it had been only for some fifteen hours and
then we were under safe escort. The crew, for whom all this was novel
and who had hardly bargained for being beset, remained quite undis-
mayed and in excellent spirits. What, I wondered, would the crew of
the previous year have made of it?

We needed to be always on the alert, fending off or warping out of
danger, the situation changing almost from hour to hour. It was surprising how floes, covering perhaps half an acre, could be persuaded
to move away a little by steady shoving. We were not vigilant enough.
A small floe drifted under the counter and by jamming the rudder
hard over broke our beautiful carved, wooden tiller, the pride of the
ship. We had a spare iron tiller which we now got ready but for safety's sake did not fit until our escape from the ice. Icebergs were the
greatest menace. The pack, and *Sea Breeze* with it, was moving steadily
north-west with the current at the rate of about one knot. The bergs,
drawing several hundred more feet, were unaffected or perhaps felt a
counter-current, so that we had the impression that they were moving
in the opposite direction at a similar speed, brushing aside everything
in their path and causing all the ice within a quarter mile of them to
jostle and gyrate. Here, then, was some danger of pressure. Any berg
to the north of us we watched apprehensively, striving to determine its
course and whether or not this would prove to be a collision course.
Happily, none of them passed within a quarter of a mile, and great
was our relief when they had drawn abeam and then safely astern. One

monster, some 200 yards long and 50 yards wide, resembled an aircraft carrier steaming majestically by, complete with flight-deck, bridge, and funnel.

By July 10th we were well north of the Frederikshaab glacier and abeam of some skerries two or three miles off to which I took a bearing. In two hours' time the bearing had altered ninety degrees which, if our distance off was correct, gave us a speed of one knot. Besides this coastal navigation I also tried some celestial navigation, though with a horizon of ice the results had to be used with caution. I took a meridian sight from up the shrouds in order to cancel out the height of the ice on the horizon. It put us in Lat. 62° 53′ N. opposite Fiskenaesset, or eighty miles north-west of Frederikshaab. We were certainly getting on, though not in the right direction. The day being windless I took another sight of the sun reflected in a little pool of perfectly still water alongside, halving the angle so found. It agreed approximately with the first sight. Later, on our way to Arsuk, on a foggy day with a bright sun overhead, we tried the same dodge using a tin of oil on deck, with results so erratic as to be useless.

Some of us used to take a daily walk, pacing our ice lawn back and forth twenty times to accomplish a mile. There was a good pool of melt-water lying on the floe from which we replenished our tanks, the water being perfectly fresh. The Arctic Pilot gives the reason:

> The enclosed brine in frozen sea water is itself seldom frozen; it tends to sink through the surrounding crystal network on account of its density being greater than that of the ice. With the summer rise of temperature the process is more rapid, and level ice, as the young ice of this age should be called, may lose almost all its salt content. If there is hummocking the progress is again speeded up and a single summer is enough for the ice to become fresh. No taste of salt can be detected by taste and ice of this nature is a source of the purest possible drinking water.

The weather was as usual mixed—fog, rain, drizzle, even one flawless day of unbroken sunshine when an aeroplane and a helicopter flew low over the ice. No doubt they were taking advantage of the weather to fly an ice patrol and we sincerely hoped we had not been spotted, later to be involuntarily rescued. It might be thought that had any of us had the wit to understand a little Danish we might have benefited, or at least kept out of danger, by listening to the ice reports broadcast daily by Godthaab radio and local stations. To make use of such information we would, of course, have to know where we were, but apart from that there is always the time lag and the rapid changes that take place in the ice picture. And, as we have seen, the infrequency of weather clear enough for ice patrols to be flown must affect the accuracy of the reports.

By July 13th, another foggy day, we could detect signs of a loosening of the ice. Later, when the fog thinned, we could see a lot of open water inshore of us. Next morning, to avoid the pressing attentions of a neighbouring floe, we carried out what proved to be our last warping manoeuvre. The fog then cleared, disclosing nothing but scattered floes to the eastward, and after a hasty lunch we cast off from our faithful friend. After motoring to get clear we set all plain sail and sped north-eastwards in more or less open water.

A passing fishing boat ignored us, but presently we sighted a small coaster coming our way. Having about reached the navigator's nadir of having to ask a passing ship where he is, we hove to and hoisted our ensign, whereupon, after circling round, he came alongside and we passed him our lines. The crew were Greenlanders, deaf and dumb so far as we were concerned, but the skipper, a young Dane, spoke good English. He was delighted to see us, delighted, that is, to see so strange a sight as a boat under sail in those waters. In the wheelhouse I had a good look at his large-scale chart. Faeringehavn was our nearest port, twenty miles distant, north by east magnetic, and no ice. Our five-day drift in the pack of just about 100 miles had carried us off my large-scale charts. I had brought no charts for north of Frederikshaab, never thinking we should find ourselves even that far north. Having inspected *Sea Breeze* and passed over a case of Carlsberg—refusing any gift in return—the Dane went on his way to Fiskenaesset. That night, instead of enjoying the bright lights of Faeringehavn, we were once more hove to in fog and a bitter north-west wind dodging stray ice floes. Pasta and stewed apples.

CHAPTER XIII

TO JULIANEHAAB

O FF FAERINGEHAVN NEXT MORNING, without a chart for the entrance, we relied upon the directions in the Pilot. These are usually, perhaps intentionally, full of foreboding, and those for Faeringehavn were no exception. 'The entrance to Faeringehavn, which is encumbered with islets and shoals, etc., etc... No vessel should attempt to enter the harbour without local knowledge.' The key to a safe entrance seemed to be Sorre Sker, described in the Pilot as 'a small rock with an orange circular mark painted on it, as the beacon is frequently destroyed during gales.' While looking for this rock we hove to, and a Canadian vessel, *Blue Cloud*, which then appeared from northwards, hove to for the same reason. He, too, was a stranger in these parts. On the principle of always putting the stranger nearest the danger we proposed letting him lead the way and had to keep the engine going flat out to keep him in sight. Just as he made his last turn, which happened to be the wrong one, a bank of fog came down. There are three harbours; a very small basin serving the administrative part of the town, the fishing and commercial harbour a mile up the fjord, and the oiling jetty south of the fjord. *Blue Cloud*'s skipper had mistakenly entered the first and had great trouble turning round to extricate himself. When he was out of the way we went there, too, to make our number with the officials and to post letters, before moving on to the main harbour.

We lay at the end of a long quay where the local fishing boats were busy discharging their catch for sale to the Norwegian-owned fish factory on the quay. The catch was almost exclusively cod. Our thoughts were centred on salmon but there were none to be had. While we were there the first boat of the season left to take part in the controversial deep-sea salmon fishing which is thought likely to lead to a big diminution of the salmon running up European rivers, our own rivers in particular. We were told that the fishing starts on the Baffin-Island side of Davis Strait and follows the salmon as they head for the Greenland rivers later in the season. A Norwegian-owned fish factory is something new, for until 1950 all Greenland activities were the monopoly of the state-owned Royal Greenland Trading Company; now, even in small ports, there are privately owned shops and supermarkets. At a so-called 'Boutique' in Faeringehavn I bought two large-scale charts. At the Sailor's Home, a common feature of Icelandic ports but rare in Greenland, we had showers and substantial meals. Shipping gossip travels fast in Greenland. On the evening of our arrival I had a pleasant surprise in the form of a signal from a Danish friend, Captain Stamphøj, sent from his ship then homeward-bound forty miles west of Faeringehavn, congratulating us on our safe arrival in Greenland. The owner of a small motor boat lying alongside us had with him two paying passengers, Danish ornithologists. Armed with binoculars and expensive cameras they were working their way down the coast bird-watching.

Having come or been driven so far north I was tempted to take the easy course by going on to Godthaab, the capital of Greenland only thirty miles away, and to the many mountainous fjords further north. We would have met no ice and would have had more climbing, but by now Julianehaab, lurking behind its ice barrier, held something of a challenge. At first we thought of following the coast down, taking advantage of the lead of open water supposedly to be found between the ice and the shore. From our later experience we found that this 'open' water contained large quantities of ice, and a passage with innumerable islets, skerries, and rocks awash on the one hand, and pack-ice on the other, is not at all inviting. We happened to meet on the wharf a Danish naval officer, Captain Jacobsen, whose ship was then taking on oil. He took Colin and me off to her. There was no question of being piped over the side or of saluting the quarter-deck, if that is what naval etiquette demands, for the only way of getting on board was by climbing monkey-fashion along a mooring warp. The ship, a large frigate or a small cruiser, could not be accommodated alongside the jetty. Over drinks the captain showed us the latest ice reports, by which he did not set great store, and finally advised us to go right out to sea clear of the ice and then to sail south-east as far as the latitude of Arsuk where he was confident that by then the ice would be navigable.

Accordingly on the 17th, having stocked up with black bread and received a present of six large cod from a happily drunken Faeroe islander, we moved to the oil wharf where we took on sixty gallons of diesel oil and 10 gallons of paraffin. A mile or two outside the entrance a line of white seemed to suggest impenetrable ice until one got close to it. Looked at from afar from a small boat all ice looks alike, one has to get really close in order to see whether or not it is navigable. In this instance the ice proved no hindrance and as we left the coast astern it became steadily less. After some eighteen miles of motoring we hoisted sail in open water but with the barometer falling from 1010 mbs. to 994 mbs. in a matter of hours, trouble might be expected. By evening we were hove to for a short-lived gale-force blast. Even when hove to *Sea Breeze* moves crab-wise quite fast and by midnight we had come up with some unexpected ice to the west. Hove to on the other tack heading east, we spent the rest of a dirty, wet night dodging small floes and growlers. So far out in Davis Strait, or in dire straits as Colin called them, we had not bargained for this.

With less than 200 miles to go to reach the latitude of Arsuk, four days in the open sea should have been enough. Thanks to fog, heavy and sometimes prolonged rain, head winds and calms, we took ten days. Five days elapsed before I could even take a sight, and that put us no less than 120 miles out from the coast. A fair wind then gave us a good shove and on the 24th, in the accustomed fog, we heard once more the growl of pack-ice close to the south-east. The next day, remarkable for excellent visibility, we rounded the northern edge of this ice and steered for a point where some far distant ice-blink appeared to end. The ice hereabouts was in the form of large fields or rafts that had broken away from the main body, and given clear weather, they could be avoided. A temptingly deep bay of open water lay all along our starboard hand but beyond it the sky showed the pronounced blink of more ice. This ice-blink is a valuable guide, just as in tropic seas a pale green light in the sky may betray the presence of a lagoon. The Arctic Pilot thus describes it:

The ice-blink is quite unmistakable over solid and extensive pack. On clear days, with the sky mostly blue, ice-blink appears as a luminous yellow haze on the horizon in the direction of the ice. On

Sailing in Torssukatak Fjord

days with overcast skies or low clouds the yellow colour is mostly absent, the blink appearing as a whitish glare on the clouds. In fog, white patches indicate the presence of ice at a short distance. When approaching pack-ice or when wholly or mainly surrounded by it, the band of ice-blink may be sharply broken by one or more dark patches known as water sky. These indicate the direction of leads or open water. If low on the horizon, water-sky may possibly indicate the presence of open water up to as much as 40 miles beyond the visible horizon.

To pick out all these signs infallibly would need a life-time of experience. All is not ice that blinks.

Frequent climbs had to be made to the cross-trees whence one surveyed the sea and the sky to judge as best one could the course to steer. We should have had a crow-nest fitted, and to make life easier—which is the aim of everyone nowadays—such a one as I saw on the *Kista Dan*, an Antarctic relief ship. It was heated, closed all round with glass (fitted with windscreen wipers), and could be reached without exposing oneself to the air by means of a ladder *inside* the mast. Still steering east we were at last brought up short by a barrier of ice that apparently could not be turned. Open water lay beyond, as we could see from aloft, and since the ice was barely a mile in width we chose the weakest spot and gingerly sneaked our way through. On the weather side, where the swell rocked the floes up and down, *Sea Breeze* sustained some hard knocks; in fact by now the water-line planks had bristles like a toothbrush but as yet the hull had suffered no serious damage.

By evening we came up with what looked like the main body of the pack and since we were still too far north we followed it south during the night for about forty miles. We saw a whale and a seal, and had our usual Sunday supper of curry and a duff swimming in treacle. Having run our distance by the morning we headed boldly eastwards into the ice, only the windward edge at all thick, and navigable even under sail as we got further in. Between drifting banks of fog I managed to take a reliable noon sight which put us plumb on the desired latitude. All afternoon and evening we chugged on—the wind had died—through scattered floes, fog all round and blue sky overhead, until I began to

doubt that Greenland did in fact lie ahead. At last at 11 p.m. the land
loomed up and we came to anchor off what I earnestly hoped was Sermersut Island at the entrance to Arsuk fjord. It is 3150 feet high and
the summit, if one can see it, is serrated. In our haste to have done we
had anchored in the first likely looking cove. It had an uneven rocky
bottom and was occupied by a large floe, so we got the anchor up and
moored to a convenient floe in mid-fjord. As we were having a night-
cap of tea and rum the watch on deck reported lights to the north. If
we really were off Sermersut no lights, either of a settlement or of a
navigational aid, could possibly be seen.

In the morning we made out a cluster of radio masts high up on
a headland five miles to the north. At first I thought of going there
where, in the course of casual conversation, we might learn where we
were without the shame of asking. But the more I looked at the lie of
the land the more assured I was that we were in the right fjord. The
crew remained sceptical until after motoring eastwards a few miles we
spotted a beacon, convincing evidence that we were right for Arsuk.
The beacons marking the recognised channels through the fjords con-
sist of a small red or yellow triangle mounted on a 10 foot-high metal
staff. If the triangle points downwards the beacon is left to starboard
and vice versa. The radio masts we had seen, ignored on the chart,
were evidently a link in some Early Warning or tracking system. Since
they are conspicuous enough from seaward they might as well figure
on the chart.

We passed the small settlement of Arsuk without stopping and
went on another ten miles to Ivigtut. Our first day in the fjords was
enjoyably summer-like. We sat on deck sunning ourselves and tracing
imaginary routes up the almost sheer rock walls on either hand, walls
that at one point were less than a cable apart. So far the weather
had been unkind but in the fjords there was a marked improvement;
there is far less fog in the fjords than at sea, and the further inland
the fjord penetrates the better the weather. Over the ice-cap the sky
seemed to be always blue. I may be wrong, but I believe that to
enjoy hot, summer weather in Greenland one needs to be north of
the Arctic Circle.

I felt a little nervous about entering Ivigtut. The Pilot has this
warning:

> Vessels are forbidden to enter Arsuk fjord until permission has been obtained immediately before entry from the Cryolite Mine Administration and every vessel must display her national flag while proceeding through the fjord and while approaching and entering Arsuk and Ivigtut roadsteads.

Accordingly on arrival, not wishing to obtrude, we made for a small cove where we would be inconspicuous. The harbourmaster, who was then busy berthing a cargo vessel, took time off to rush over in his launch to shoo us away, directing us instead to a small-boat harbour where we lay alongside in the snuggest berth we had had for some time. Some Danes who came on board for a drink took the crew away for beer and smorgbrod at the club. I turned in for a long sleep.

The importance of Ivigtut lies in its cryolite mine, a rare mineral used in the aluminium industry. The only other source, I believe, is in Russia, though the stuff can be made synthetically at a price. The Ivigtut mine, a large hole in the ground now full of water, is worked out, but we were told that the ore stock would take ten years to shift at the rate of 50,000 tons a year. The mine has been worked since the last century and was discovered as long ago as 1794. In spite of intensive search no similar deposit has yet been found in Greenland, but since Greenland has a coastline of over 24,000 miles, equal to the circumference of the earth, there is room for discovery. In its palmy days the low grade ore was used for road or wharf foundations or dumped in the fjord. Some of this is now being recovered by dredging. No Greenlanders are employed at the mine and the present Danish staff is down to about fifty.

Next day I visited the cargo ship *Edith Nielsen* that had come in the previous evening. The captain told me that he had taken three days to come from Frederikshaab going dead slow all the way; he said that among floes radar was of little help. The brother of the King of Denmark, an elderly man and a director of the Royal Greenland Company, was that day to visit the mine having arrived by helicopter at the nearby naval base of Gronnedal. *Sea Breeze* has a full locker of signal flags and here was an occasion, perhaps the only one, when they might be used. So we dressed ship over all and could only hope that her gay appearance was duly noted by the Prince as he drove by in a jeep. *Edith*

Nielsen, the only other vessel there, was too busy loading cryolite to pay attention to etiquette, Danish though she was. We could obtain no black bread, more desirable for us on account of its excellent keeping qualities. The Danes at Ivigtut had not come to Greenland to eat black bread, so the twenty loaves that had been ordered for us from their bakery were white. They were so good and vanished so quickly that mould never had a chance to start. We took on more fuel because for the remainder of our time we would be using the engine a lot in the fjords, and since we would be in fjords we could afford to carry a drum on deck. We got this 40 gal. drum in exchange for a bottle of gin. Torsukatak, the fjord we had originally aimed at, was now the objective, and we reached it by way of an inshore passage through the skerries, meeting little ice and using sails for part of the time. Just south of the entrance to Torsukatak is Cape Desolation, so named by John Davis in 1585, 'the most deformed, rockie, mountainous land that ever we saw… and the shore beset with yce a league off into the sea, making such yrksome noyse as that it seemed to be the true pattern of desolation.'

We anchored for the night inside the fjord at a recognised anchorage called Bangshavn where we caught a few cod. Cod of 3 to 4 lb. weight, enough for our needs, could be caught at most of our fjord anchorages by dangling any kind of lure a few feet up from the bottom. For a long time, until we got sick of the sight of them and threw them overboard, we had cod hung from the boom gallows drying in the hope that they would be eaten on the voyage home. From Torsukatak we entered Bredefjord, wide and long, extending some forty-five miles inland from Julianehaab Bight to terminate close to the ice-cap. Halfway up the fjord was a mountain we wanted to examine and also a branch fjord by which we could reach Julianehaab. Saturday August 1st was a perfect summer day with just enough wind for us to sail. We lunched lingeringly on deck in the hot sun. The wind had died and for some time we were content to drift, loath to break the profound calm by turning on the engine. We had our peak in view less than ten miles away—not very interesting, I thought, but with the days slipping by and no mountain yet climbed Colin and Iain were champing at the bit.

Right from the start the fjord had been moderately strewn with floes and icebergs and their numbers now began to increase. For some time we had been going dead slow, threading a most tortuous course through ever thickening ice, and twice I had predicted that the next opening ahead would prove to be the last and that we were wasting our time. At last even Colin, at whose pressing urge we still persevered, had to admit defeat in the face of a high, unbroken wall of floes and bergs stretching from shore to shore. We were then a short mile from Narsaq, a settlement in the branch fjord, and behind which lay our mountain. Some of this ice may have come from the ice-cap at the head of the fjord but most of it was probably the result of the meeting of the two fjords and the fact that at this point Bredefjord had narrowed to less than a mile wide. So with a wasted day behind us we rethreaded our way through the mass of ice to find an anchorage for the night in a less crowded part of the fjord. There was a lot of weed on the bottom in many of the fjord anchorages and we gave up using the CQR in favour of our heavy Fisherman-type anchor. Baked potatoes, sausage and French beans.

I regretted our not having visited Narsaq, the place the Vikings called Dyrnes, where there are the ruins of several of their homesteads and a church. In the ruins of one of the homesteads was found a runic staff, reputedly the oldest yet found in Greenland and said to date from the time of Erik the Red, *circa* 986. Erik's own homestead was at Brattalid in the next fjord south of Narsaq and about twenty miles away. The so-called Eastern settlement stretched from Torsukatak Fjord in the south up to Ivigtut, and in it the remains of 190 farms, twelve churches, a cathedral, and a monastery have been identified. In the Western settlement, concentrated around Godthaab Fjord, there were ninety farms and 4 churches. It is thought that in its hey-day there were some 3000 Norse settlers, all from Iceland. As well as making the Vinland voyages from Greenland they seem to have ranged far to the north, probably on hunting expeditions—to Upernivik in Lat. 73° N., for example, where in 1824 an Eskimo found a stone inscribed with runes telling that in 1333 three Norsemen had wintered there; and cairns, thought to have been built by Norsemen, have been found in Jones Sound 76° N., and near Ellesmere Island in 79° N.

While much is known about the Viking settlements, what still remains obscure is how and why they vanished from history. Various theories have been advanced but for none of them is there any real evidence; that they died out through physical degeneration; that they died of the plague, the Black Death that ravaged Norway in 1349; that in the face of pressure from the Eskimos moving southwards they migrated to the adjacent parts of Canada; that they blended with the Eskimo and disappeared as a separate race, or that the Eskimos exterminated them. The Greenland carrier made its last voyage in 1369 and in 1406 the last vessel known to have reached Greenland arrived there by mistake and did not get away for four years. The rest is silence. In his *History of the Vikings* Professor Gwyn Jones sums up:

> In the present state of knowledge it seems safest to conclude that the Greenland colony died out for no one reason but through a complex of deadly pressures. Of these its isolation from Europe, the neglect it suffered from its northern kinsmen, the lack of trade and new blood, the worsening conditions of cold, and above all the encroaching Eskimo, were the most important. Even in theory they sound more than enough to bring down the curtain on this farthest medieval outpost of what had been the Viking, and was now the European world, and extinguish it with all the trappings of inexorable and heart-chilling doom.

After a long day, fog all morning and rain all afternoon, we anchored short of Julianehaab in Motzfeldthavn. As I had spent all day on deck, puzzling over the intricate windings of the passage and looking out for beacons, the crew stood by anchor watch. Fishing whiled away the tedium of anchor watches and overnight the crew caught between them a fine lot of cod. Next day, August 3rd, some three weeks behind schedule, we reached Julianehaab. We secured first alongside a local boat where we were immediately overrun by a swarm of small Greenlanders who, having pried into everything on board, settled down on deck to jig for cod. For the sake of quiet we removed the children and went to an anchorage among a fleet of small craft.

Compared with Godthaab, the town is modest enough and it is not easy to see why a place that is not easy to reach, especially in summer, should be of importance, except that it is in the centre of the sheep-farming region. In Greenland there are no roads outside the townships, yet in Julianehaab, where one could walk from one end to the other in ten minutes, there are numerous cars and even taxis. There are plenty of shops and in one we all bought anoraks which seemed good and cheap; all, that is, except Colin who of course makes his own. There was even a well-stocked bookshop where Iain and I both invested in an expensive illustrated account of the life of Jakob Danielsen, a famous Greenland hunter and artist who lived at Godhavn up by Disko Island and died in 1938. In it there are many delightful drawings and water-colours portraying hunting scenes and the Eskimo way of life throughout the year.

That evening we were whisked away by speedboat to visit an experimental farm ten miles away up the fjord. The sheep—of Icelandic stock—were out on the hill but we saw the stables where they are housed in winter, and the few acres of Rye and Timothy grass that provided their winter keep. In a large nursery potatoes, cabbage, and carrots were doing well while radish, a cool-climate product if ever there was one, waxed fat. Rhubarb, which we had noticed growing outside a few houses in Julianehaab, would not win any prizes for giant sticks, but at least it grows. Strawberries were growing under glass and looked well, but the young trees, mostly conifers, were not thriving. In the absence of forests, the forest officer, whom we met, has a discouraging job. He had been there for seventeen years and consoled himself with a Greenlander wife, a large family, and homebrewed beer—lacking a little in head, but clear, amber, and hoppy. I speak as a home-brewer.

CHAPTER XIV

TO THE MOUNTAINS

———————◆———————

To reach Tasermiut, the fjord where we hoped to find some good mountains, we skirted the inside of Julianehaab Bight, keeping generally inside the numerous islands and skerries. These serve as only a partial barrier to the ice in the Bight outside; like water, ice-floes seem to penetrate the merest cracks. We set out on an overcoat afternoon having first gone alongside to fill up with water and to collect forty loaves of black bread. Once outside Julianehaab Fjord we were among floes where two hunters in kayaks were prowling about on the look-out for seals. On that grey day the scene reminded me of the drawings in my Jakob Danielsen book. In this part of Greenland seals are not plentiful and kayaks are rare. Yet they are regularly hunted and at the smaller settlements we would be offered skins, usually at a staggering price. Bob and Andrew bought their sealskins at a shop, dressed skins that had been to Copenhagen and back. They were small and comparatively cheap. The skins offered to us at the settlements were mostly prime specimens that may have been in the family for years pending the arrival of suckers and tourists like ourselves.

We anchored that night near the tip of a horseshoe-shaped island, the two arms enclosing a wide reach of water, and from the shore of our little bay the ground ran up to a col 200 or 300 feet high. No reassuring anchorage symbol appeared on the chart but it looked safe, reasonably snug, and almost free of ice. Throughout the next day fog held us prisoners there and towards evening the barometer dropped quickly from 1011 to 1004 mbs. Very violent gusts of wind then began to sweep down from the col, tearing up the water in sheets of spray. The anchor soon dragged. Having shortened up I tried to get the boat further into the cove but in the fierce gusts the boat's head kept falling off. Having narrowly missed hitting the rocks with the bowsprit we abandoned the cove and anchored again further inside the horseshoe, veering forty fathoms of chain at a mere thirty yards from the rocky shore.

In the big bay where the Jensens' sheep farm lay

The Jensens' house beyond the gate; sheep stabling on the right

The gusts here were perhaps slightly less violent than those sweeping down from the col which seemed to act like a wind tunnel. We kept the engine going to ease the strain on the cable, all hands stood by on deck, with a man at the tiller to meet the wild yaws that were bringing the stern horribly close to the rocks. There was no question of seeking safety outside where the Bight was full of ice. Had the anchor not held we had no other card to play short of motoring up and down in mid-reach where willie-waws danced across the water and more ice kept drifting in. With the glass rising to 10 mbs in two hours the wind began to take off and by midnight all was calm. This short-lived storm bent both palms of the anchor. Happily, we had finished supper just as the trouble started—fillets of cod with a delicate fish sauce of Andrew's invention, and mashed potatoes. As Dr Opimian said: 'Whatever happens in this world never let it spoil your dinner.'

Upon emerging next morning from this ill-starred horseshoe we were stopped by a mass of floes and bergs driven inshore by the brief gale. A few miles back on the way we had come there was an alternative route which we now went back to try. The crux was a fifty-yard wide pass between an island and the mainland where, as we now found, two big bergs had drifted in and grounded. In trying to squeeze through between the shore and one of the bergs we went aground, got off with difficulty, and withdrew to a nearby anchorage. From there we went in the dinghy to explore a similar narrow pass which proved far too shallow for *Sea Breeze*. Next day we tried the original route where we were once more foiled by a combination of ice and fog and had to spend another night in the horseshoe. The nights were by now becoming dark and for the first time we saw the Northern Lights.

At our third attempt we were doing well until mid-day when the ice became so thick that I decided to go back. Easier said than done. The oddly-shaped bergs or floes that we had noted on the way were still in sight to guide us back but the pattern of the ice in between was no longer the same, the leads by which we had come having closed. We wasted hours backing and filling in order to turn the boat round after getting stuck in some blind lead, and finally we managed to plant the boat's keel firmly astride a projecting tongue of ice. Nothing would shift her. It looked as if we would be there until the ice melted, until we resorted to the old dodge of rocking the boat by combined rushes of the crew from side to side. Though it was not the course we wanted, when a lead towards the shore offered we took it thankfully and anchored in Zacharia's Havn. We had made a good twelve miles in ten hours. Iain and Andrew bathed under a handy waterfall to the astonishment of some natives who had walked over from the nearby settlement of Sydproven. We were running short of time or we should have visited Sydproven where, according to the *Pilot*, 'the church and houses are built of stone in a style of architecture far superior to the wooden edifices usually seen in this country.'

Even on the next day we did not quite reach Tasermiut Fjord, being stopped by a sudden and furious head wind which made close steering among ice-floes altogether too hazardous. This short-lived blast came with a sharp rise in the barometer. We could only account for all these recent setbacks by the presence on board of a Jonah, and the lot fell on Abdul, the name we had given to the carved head of a coloured gentleman, Moor or Malay, who leered down on us from his place under the saloon skylight. He had a sardonic sneer and shifty eyes and had been inherited by me with the boat. We therefore committed Abdul to life on an ice-floe instead of in *Sea Breeze*'s, warm, wet saloon. Zacharia's Havn provided us with seven fine cod, and that night we witnessed another fine auroral display, great shafts of greenish light that for more than an hour waxed, waned, flickered, and finally died.

At the entrance to Tasermiut Fjord is a small township, Nanortalik, where we stopped for an hour to shop, thinking that this was our last chance before starting homewards. At Julianehaab we had been advised to call on a Mr Jensen who owned a sheep-farm in Tasermiut, so ten miles up the fjord we turned off through a narrow pass to emerge in a wide bay where at its northern end we could make out the Jensen homestead. It was a lovely bay of bright blue water and beyond the olive-green slopes that ran gently down to its shores stood a fierce array of jagged peaks. They were mostly rock and uncommonly steep. We anchored off a sandy beach on a calm, sunny evening, and had not some of the peaks been decorated with small hanging glaciers we might have been in some Highland loch. We felt we had at last got to the heart of the matter. Supper consisted of steamed fish and cabbage cooked in water with a drop of Stockholm tar that gave it a pleasing smoky flavour. Andrew garnished the fish with another sauce of

In Torssukatak Fjord

Anchored in a fjord; Iain about to dive in for a bathe
and Bob waiting to photograph the diver

his own invention that would have pleased Dr Folliot. As that worthy observed: 'The science of fish sauce is by no means brought to perfection, a fine field of discovery still lies open in that line.'

Colin and Iain having sorted out their climbing gear set off to reconnoitre a big peak overlooking the anchorage, while I walked up to the Jensen's house to introduce ourselves. Mr Jensen spoke no English and his wife only a little, haltingly. Which was unlucky because we had many questions to ask about sheep-farming in Greenland and about the Viking ruins hard by the house which we were presently shown. Expecting to see at least the remains of obvious stone walls, I was disappointed. These were, so to speak, completely ruined ruins. It needed some creative imagination to transform two holes in the ground like disused sawpits, and three straight lines of stones, into two Viking houses within their protecting walls. Nevertheless the artefacts that Mr Jensen had found on this unpromising site were convincing evidence. These were mostly weights for looms, small flat stones with holes drilled in them. More, perhaps, may have been found, for we were told that some Danish archaeologists had recently visited the site.

Strictly speaking, therefore, the Jensens were not pioneers, some unknown Viking having farmed the same land a thousand years earlier. For all that, the two holes in the ground were not much to build on and the Jensens had in fact started from scratch; housing first themselves, building stables for 400 sheep, and clearing and ploughing the ten acres from which Mr Jensen was at that moment busy harvesting rye grass for winter fodder. All this and the running of 1100 sheep was done with no help but that of two Iceland ponies and three friendly Border collies. The ponies did the ploughing and the mowing, too, if the state of the ground allowed, otherwise Mr Jensen had to use a scythe. The sheep ranged over a vast area, though strictly limited in height by the short distance up the mountain slopes that vegetation could survive. They were rounded up in the autumn and all but 400 sent away for slaughter. They were so scattered that one seldom saw any. Plodding through the dwarf willow, juniper, and heath that made walking an arduous exercise, one might come across two or three at the most, and these would immediately take to their heels like so many wild antelope.

The Jensens visited us the next evening bringing some rhubarb, radishes, and carrots. The talk—helped out by a dictionary—turned to salmon, a fish that had been on our minds for some time. A large lake two miles away was apparently full of salmon and although we had no means of catching them, the Greenlanders at a nearby settlement had, and visited the lake frequently for that purpose. In asking us to eat salmon next evening Mrs Jensen had therefore every confidence that they would be available, as indeed they were in abundance. For that memorable meal alone we reckoned the voyage had been worth while. Their house was spacious and well furnished; cooking by Calor gas and oil lamps for lighting. The only modern gadget was a radio telephone which kept them in touch with Julianehaab.

The mountaineers' first reconnaissance had been foiled by mist and they now went off in another direction to look for a suitable mountain. Colin, accustomed to New Zealand mountains, liked them with plenty of ice and none of the needle-like peaks in the vicinity seemed to offer him much chance to ply his mighty axe. While taking a stroll towards the salmon lake, a turquoise gem set amid high snow peaks, I thought I could see just what Colin wanted, a mountain about 6000 feet high abounding with ridges and shoulders, glaciers, ice-falls, snow couloirs, and névé. It lay far away at the head of the lake, but distance meant nothing to them and Colin and Iain took fire at my report.

We were enjoying a brief spell of marvellous weather when they set off for this distant peak carrying four days' food and no tent. Evidently, even in the Antipodes, the rumour has got around that armies march on their stomachs. I provided them with a couple of days' food in the form of two old tins of pemmican, a food new to Colin and one that on this trip earned his highest esteem. I gave him the Copenhagen address where it could be obtained, but he rather thought he would be making it himself, meat and fat being so plentiful in Australia. But they wanted more than this snack and as well as necessities took luxuries like flour, potatoes, currants, spaghetti, just as if they were going on a camping holiday. We had a good supply of real farmhouse cheese—no soapy, processed stuff—of which they took a liberal share. As Colin said, even if they failed on the mountain they could have a Cheddar gorge.

In their absence the ship-keepers did a lot of walking. I found my first walk to a distant tarn at about 2000 feet fatiguing and not repaying; mosquitoes and midges were maddening and I had to cross a fast-flowing and frigidly cold glacier stream. Still, the mosquitoes of southern Greenland are nothing like the torment they are further north. We also paid a visit to the lake which discharges into the fjord by way of a wide channel, hardly deserving the name of river, for it is only 200 or 300 yards long. Judging from a few small patches of smooth, rich green grass on the banks of the channel, Vikings may have lived there, too. It seemed to be a favoured spot climatically, where there were groves of birch growing to a height of twenty feet, twisted and warped by wind, but real trees.

The climbing party returned on the third day having had the worst of luck with the weather. The fine spell broke on the second day when they were on the summit ridge not far from the top, whence they were forced to retreat in a hurry before the onset of a severe storm. Nevertheless they had had some good climbing, Colin had used his brain-biter with effect, and accustomed as they were to the frustrations of New Zealand weather, defeat did not rankle. The fact remained that we had only a fortnight left and that so far we had nothing to show. We intended leaving Greenland about September 1st by way of Prins Christian Sund, the eastern end of the inland waterway that links the west to the east coast well inside Cape Farewell. The western end of the waterway is Torssukatak (two S's this time), a fjord bristling with mountains where we could profitably spend the remaining time. Having said good-bye to the kind Mr and Mrs Jensen we started back down the fjord leaving Nanortalik well on our starboard hand. As we turned south for the twenty-mile run down the coast we had a brisk wind dead astern. Frederiksdal, a small settlement at the fjord entrance, was our goal for the night. With a fair wind the boat romped along through pretty ice-free water, but with the wind aft we had to tack and in moderate visibility were seldom close enough to the shore to distinguish any beacons. At 7 p.m., having run our distance, we gybed confidently for the run in to Frederiksdal and Torssukatak Fjord. On reaching the fjord entrance we were surprised at the absence of any beacons or of any glimmer of light from the settlement. It rather looked as if someone had blundered. In the gathering gloom we stood on into the fjord where it took us another two hours to find an anchorage. In these deep fjords it is always a problem. Only at the mouth of rivers or off a valley that once held a glacier, is there much chance of finding shallow enough water. Even so one may find oneself closing the shore, the distance becoming perilously less, while the mournful cry of 'no bottom at ten' still echoes back from the leadsman.

My guess was that we were short of Frederiksdal but nothing that we had seen on the way in could be reconciled with any of the fjords as shown on the chart. As we repassed the fjord entrance on our way out to sea next morning I noticed a little hook-shaped cape which gave me an inkling of where we were and from further out I could iden-tify Cape Christian, only five miles from Cape Farewell and the end of Greenland. We had overshot our mark by two fjords. We took a beaconed short cut to Frederiksdal from which an accumulation of ice forced us to retire, and then near the settlement we luckily met a ven-erable and genial Greenlander returning in his dory with a nice catch of cod. We took him on board, made fast the dory astern, and handed him the tiller. He told us the harbour was chock-full of ice and took us instead to a place we should never have found for ourselves, a small cleft among the rocks, deep water and just room for *Sea Breeze* and not much else. To our alarm a small coasting vessel *Narwhal* now appeared evidently heading for the same hole. Her skipper turned her in her own length, backed into the gap between us and the rock wall, and having made fast to it began discharging his cargo on top of it.

The Royal Greenland Trading Company had a store here where we bought honey, lemons, coffee, and some galvanised nails for tingles. By now there were some deep gashes along the waterline that would need to be covered before leaving Greenland. Our pilot took us to his house—neat, clean, and warm—where we discussed the merits and price of a large sealskin. It was too dark in colour to be really attractive and no sale resulted. Outside most of the houses there were hanging rows of cod's heads that had been cleaned of everything except the teeth. We were told they were good for making soup—tasty, no doubt, but hardly nourishing. I should like to have had Dr Folliot's opinion. There was a dance that night in the local Town Hall, a bleak shed lit by one Aladdin lamp, and only heavy rain prevented Bob and Andrew from attending.

Motoring next day up Torssukatak we met *Narwhal* on her way back from the even smaller settlement of Augpilagtoq, the last in southern Greenland. We stopped short of it at a marked anchorage called Stordalens havn close to a 6000-foot peak that looked extremely difficult, steep and probably rotten rock as most of it is in those parts. We were roused out early by an intruding floe that obliged us to move twice before it went on its way. I went up to a snow col at about 2500 feet to spy out the land and I got the impression that some of the formidable rock towers in the vicinity would go if approached from the ice-cap side as opposed to the fjord side. There were difficulties about that, too, for the snow basin to which the col gave access was cut off from the ice-cap by a high rock wall. Coming back, hot and sweaty, I had a far from memorable bathe in a shallow runnel and had a long walk across flats of hard sand to reach the water, the tide being out. Several big floes were sitting high and dry on the sand which was thick with worm-casts. The mixture of ice-floes and worms struck me as incongruous and I wondered what Darwin, who wrote a monograph on worms, would have said of it.

Colin was temporarily 'crook', as they say in New Zealand, so that for once time spent on reconnaissance was wasted. We decided to move on, a large iceberg drifting down on us providing an immediate spur to action. In backing away too hastily from this menace we ran hard aground and had to wait for the tide to refloat us. Clearly it was not our day. On the way to Augpilagtoq, with supper long overdue, we were tempted to anchor short of the place in a bit of a cove. Some small pieces of ice drifting by showed that there was a fast current. No sooner was the anchor down in eleven fathoms than a much weightier bit of ice drifted athwart the anchor chain and hung there, threatening to break both it and the bob-stay. By going full astern and winching in cable at the same time we shook it off but not before both the shank and fluke of the anchor had been bent.

The harbour at Augpilagtoq is a long, narrow cleft in the rocks into which it seemed unlikely that any floes would drift, yet even there we were pestered by them. If there were any traffic other than small boats it would be easy and worth while to stretch a wire across the entrance as is done at Angmagssalik to keep out ice. Besides the usual cod hung out on drying racks, we were surprised to see a lot of what looked like seal blubber; forty miles or more from the sea in either direction seemed a long way inland for seals. At this small place, with a population of a hundred at most, an enterprising Greenlander had opened a café. He entertained us to coffee and biscuits while Bob entertained an audience of two small Greenlanders with the guitar that was part of the café furnishing. I paid in kind with a packet of English matches with which he was delighted.

Near Augpilagtoq three fjords meet in a broad stretch of water called Ilua. Taking advantage of a sunny day and a little wind we sailed about in Ilua while Bob and Andrew in the dinghy took photographs. That done we went on up an arm of the fjord called Kangikitsoq where we at last found an anchorage that was free of ice. Entering this arm we passed an immense piece of ice. What name it deserved, whether floe or berg, was hard to determine, for it was perfectly tabular, measured a good hundred yards either way, and was about twenty feet high. This monster was still drifting quietly to and fro in the same place when we left and promised to survive at least another summer if not two. Whence it could have come was another puzzle. Hard by, a big glacier descending from the ice-cap pushed out well into the fjord, but it looked far too wrinkled and crevassed to be the source of such a perfectly flat and symmetrical piece of ice. We looked at this glacier to see if it might provide a route up on to the ice-cap whence the climbers might have found a way up the highest peak in the fjord. It was far too broken, so we returned to our ice-free anchorage where we remained until sailing day, August 30th.

CHAPTER XV

HOMEWARD BOUND

A FTER A LONG WALK UP THE MAIN VALLEY Colin and Iain reported having found a good camp site at the foot of a glacier by which, they thought, an attractive peak could be reached. Taking five days' food and a tent they left next day for what sounded like an idyllic spot, juniper wood for a fire, a small tarn for water, the glacier highway beckoning them onward and upward. The ship-keeping party settled down to work and short walks. Bob and I spent most of the time working on the deck, gouging out any soft wood and putting in graving pieces, hammering in caulking cotton and pouring pitch into the seams. Colin had already put tingles over the deeper gashes along the water-line, but below that, where we could see there was some damage, nothing could be done. In the calm waters of the fjord she made hardly any water and although in the open sea the story might be different I did not think the case warranted our trying to beach her in order to get at problematical leaks. Most of these wounds, I regret to say, were self-inflicted, that is to say by misjudging the width of a gap between floes or by moving too fast when we should have been going dead slow, we had too often given poor *Sea Breeze* some terrible and avoidable knocks.

Andrew took up archaeology, having found what he thought was an old house site. With my ice-axe—which I implored him not to break—he delved away industriously and at length unearthed a piece of wood that looked suspiciously like part of a soap box, evidently of the post-viking period. I took a walk up the main valley, crossed the river, and came back on the other side among some of the largest boulders I have ever seen. Some of them offered the weary traveller a fine bivouac and they had evidently been used as such, judging by the rough stone walls that some bygone occupant had hoped would keep out the draught. But what would bring anyone to this valley? Salmon in the river? There are no reindeer to hunt in this part of Greenland, and we saw nowhere the least sign of life except the spoor of what was

157

probably a fox. I reached the fjord again so far from the boat that I had
to light a signal fire to summon the dinghy. On a pleasant grass flat
near the shore was a hut, probably some Greenlander's fishing lodge,
and, more interesting, a line of man-laid stones. I thought them far
superior to those at the Jensens' farm, but instead of being in a straight
line the stones were laid in a graceful curve for a length of some fifty
yards. Laid, possibly, by a deformed Viking, one leg shorter than the
other.

The climbing party returned after four days having had plenty of
fun but no great success. So late in the season snow conditions were
becoming unsafe. They had found the névé beyond their glacier highway so seamed with crevasses, and their snow bridges so frail, that they
considered it dangerous, especially for a party of only two when if one
falls in there is not enough hauling power available to get him out.
Accordingly we decided to leave as arranged on August 30th. Our ice-
free anchorage lost its good name on the morning we left when a great
floe drifted in to settle down almost alongside.

We had nearly forty miles of motoring to reach the eastern end of
Prins Christian Sund where there is a Danish weather station at which
we intended to call. This long passage is spectacular and in sunless
weather a little grim, the rock walls of the fjord extending for mile
upon mile, their continuity broken but rarely by the steep ice-fall of
a glacier cascading down from the ice-cap. Not only was the day sunless but a canopy of cloud accentuated the gloom by concealing the
heights and leaving nothing to be seen but a few hundred feet of for-
bidding rock wall lapped by steel-grey water. Some fifteen miles from
the weather station we met a small speedboat driven by two cheerful
young Danes bound for the bright lights of Augpilagtoq, the café and
the guitar. At the rate they were going it would not take long always
provided they failed to hit a small piece of ice. They must have a girl
friend there, more likely several, because they insisted on giving us two
out of a collection of large chocolate boxes stowed under their canopy.

We did not make the weather station that night. We anchored
on the south side of the fjord having inspected and discarded a more
attractive spot on the north side owing to the amount of ice there. It
was strange to be thus still pestered by ice so late in the summer when
there was practically no ice coming down with the East Greenland

At the Danish weather station

Bob fending off a small bergy bit

current. Presumably this ice was mostly debris from the local glaciers most of which came right down to the fjord. Next morning we
anchored close inshore near the little wharf of the weather station, the
vicinity of the wharf itself apparently so encumbered with rocks that
we funked going alongside. However, a reception party on the wharf
waved us in so we crept nervously into the smallest harbour I have
ever seen. But there was deep water alongside and just enough room
between the wharf and a rock wall to warp the boat round, as we did
later to make our exit easier.

The chief of the station came on board and we had barely finished
a second round of drinks before a fork-lift truck, summoned apparently by telepathy, began shovelling crates and cartons of food on
to our deck. Potatoes, long-life milk, eggs, cheese, hams, wrapped
bread, biscuits, sauces, shrimps, honey, jam, in endless variety until, I
think, we had more food on board than on the day we left Lymington.
From experience I suspected that something of the sort might happen
and had hinted as much to the crew, but I was quite taken aback by
the enormity of the happening. With one exception, these far-flung
establishments, whether in the Arctic or the sub-Antarctic, especially
if they are not British, have always been excessively kind to visitors
like myself. This station was manned by sixteen Danes who do a two-
year stint and are sustained by the most modern conveniences, showers, sauna baths, and real water closets, the only ones of their kind in
Greenland. They are well paid during their exile, as they deserve to be,
for they lead a monotonous life with no high days or holidays. One
would need to have an indoor hobby or an outdoor activity such as
ski-ing in winter and perhaps sailing in summer. Throughout the year
they get mail every three weeks from Nanortalik because in winter the
fjords do not freeze over. But this year their first supply ship arriving
from eastwards had not been able to get in until August 14th. She was,
by the way, *Britannia*, the same ship that *Mischief* had followed through
the ice to Angmagssalik in 1964.

A flight of wooden steps, several hundred of them I should guess,
led from the wharf to the main establishment on the headland. A wire-
rope railway hauled up supplies. After sampling the showers we had
drinks in a large, well-furnished ante-room before adjourning for
supper in an equally large dining hall. The cook had two assistants.

One felt that he needed them, especially on that evening when he had to provide for my crew of cormorants, worthy descendants of Carlyle's 'gluttonous race of Jutes and Angles who saw the sun rise with no other hope but that they should fill their bellies before it set.' Most of the Danes whom we met enjoyed their life in Greenland but few regarded the country as anything but an incubus, a financial incubus on the back of Denmark that they would be better without. A great deal of money has been spent in the past, and is still being spent, almost entirely for the benefit of the 30,000 or so Greenlanders who by now would be hard put to it to support themselves if support from Denmark were withdrawn. Inevitably their former self-sufficient life of bare subsistence has vanished, to be replaced by a life in which food, clothing, and other necessities have to be bought with cash.

Instead of porridge, that well-tried belly-timber, Andrew could now provide what might be called a hotel breakfast—fruit-juice, cornflakes, and real milk. After which we cast off and sailed out to sea. In a bitter north-east wind accompanied by flurries of snow we watched the desolate coast recede. By now, even on this coast, all the ice had vanished, all but some bergs that had grounded on a reef three miles out. These, the last we were to see, managed to give me a final fright. Until we had drawn near I did not appreciate how fast we were being set down on them, what with leeway and current, and that if we ran the boat off we would pile up on the reef to leeward of them. We should have gone about but by dint of sailing hard on the wind we scraped by with little enough to spare. We were going fast and by evening had got clear of the East Greenland current, as we could tell when the sea temperature rose from 35° F. at mid-day to 47° F. at 6 p.m.

As expected, the amount of pumping required increased suddenly from forty strokes to 200 strokes a watch, and next day in a rising easterly wind to over 300 strokes. By evening the wind had backed north-east and risen to a gale, the glass having fallen from 1010 mbs. to 986 mbs. Once more I was reminded of Lecky's warning, that a falling barometer with a northerly wind conveys a warning which cannot be disregarded with impunity. Throughout the night vicious squalls of wind and rain drove at us without intermission. Not wanting to lose ground to the west by running, we were hove to with everything close-reefed. The leak naturally increased, so much so that in one hour 500 strokes were needed to clear the well. This alarmed me considerably and we set double watches, one man on deck and the other pumping. By morning the wind began to take off but Andrew and Colin, unused to this rough treatment after so long a spell in calm waters, were not at all themselves. We searched diligently for a leak that, short of stripping the lining, looked like worrying us for the rest of the voyage. Two days later, however, poking about under the floorboards near the 'heads', Colin discovered a small stream coming in where a plank had started away from a frame. By fitting a strongback, and shoving oakum and tallow between plank and frame before tightening up, he practically stopped it. Easy enough to describe but the job took two days of hard work.

Three days later we had another gale, happily from northwest so that with only the staysail set we ran before it at five knots; and hardly had that blow subsided before it piped up again from north, the squalls becoming increasingly violent as the barometer rose. We reefed down successively until there were so many rolls on the boom that only about six feet of the mainsail's luff remained hoisted, but by afternoon we had to take the sail down altogether and run under bare poles, still doing three knots. We did well to hand the sail. As we got it in we saw that the gaff was badly sprung about a third of the way along from the peak. Nothing could be done at the moment, nor did we have any present use for the mainsail, the gale continuing to blow all the next day.

In all this rough weather, despite our having stopped the leak, she still made a lot of water, most of it by way of the deck where there was always water sloshing about. Certainly things were a bit damp below. The chart table, where the chronometer watch in its wooden case was screwed down, and the sextant on a shelf above, suffered from constant drips. The horizon glass of the sextant began to mist over and became progressively worse so that before the end of the voyage the sun needed to be bright to be seen at all in the mirror. Star sights were out of the question. Worse still, the winding spring of the deck watch broke. I took the time by Colin's wristwatch which was pretty steady, backed up by frequent time signals. When the wind moderated we set the topsail as a sort of trysail and with the winds remaining in a westerly quarter we made good progress. As soon as the sea had gone down and the boat steadied, Colin began sawing up a fourteen-foot length of 9-inch by 3-inch timber, exulting, I think, in having foreseen some such occasion when this great baulk of wood he had so long treasured would be put to use. In order to select the best of it he began by ripping the whole fourteen feet lengthways, a task that took a whole morning. He had already made two iron brackets and, having got his two 7-foot lengths, was able to fish the gaff.

So far we had met only two ships, both Russian, one of which altered course to have a close look at us while the crew waved and took photographs. We were then some 500 miles from the Bishop Rock where we wanted to make our landfall. That night a large bird alighted on Bob's head as he sat in the cockpit steering, Colin, the bird-fancier, was safely asleep so we put the bird in a box in the saloon hoping that when he got up to go on watch the bird would either crow or peck at him. Except that it was not a domestic fowl—though almost as big—none of us knew enough about birds to identify it. It was a queer bird, quite tame and seemingly familiar with the boat, and judging by the sardonic glint in its eye my opinion was that Abdul had adopted this disguise in order to fly from his ice-floe to haunt us. I could imagine him chewing the matter over, pondering ways and means, what disguise would best serve, and perhaps receiving inspiration for his plan from some lines he had heard me quote:

> The feathered race with pinions cleave the air;
> Not so the mackerel, and still less the bear.

When I showed the bird's photograph—he liked being photographed—to a knowledgeable friend he at once identified it as a juvenile, or immature, as the ornithologist would say, Icelandic gull. In spite of its immaturity it knew it was on to a good thing and stayed with us for two days while we fed it on pilchards and Greenland shrimps. Then one dark night he suddenly vanished. I suspect Colin could have told us why.

By the 15th we were once more under full sail, and a near gale on the following day thoroughly tested Colin's handiwork. Personally I never had any doubts, the fished gaff appearing strong enough to withstand a hurricane. This blow, for which the barometer hardly moved, went on for two days while the shipping forecast handed out gale warnings for each of the twenty-three areas it covers except for those in the

Channel. Being then well south of Mizzen Head we were quite content
to put up with the windless day that followed the gale, since it was so
gloriously fine. With so much of our gear hung out to dry the boat
looked like a second- or third-hand clothes shop. Happy in our igno-
rance, we could not know that this fine day marked the beginning of a
spell of anti-cyclonic weather that was to prevail over the British Isles
for the next fortnight, a fortnight of easterly winds and thick weather.

After breakfast on the morning of the 20th I got a sight that put
us ten miles west of the Bishop Rock and two hours later I sighted the
lighthouse fine on the starboard bow, all the islands to the north of it
hidden in fog. The crew began comparing me with Henry the Navigator, but even my own modest impression that I was becoming moderately competent in this difficult art had, within the next twenty-four
hours, to be revised.

With the wind at east we steered south to clear the islands, and
that evening in fog, visibility about 500 yards, when we were back on
the other tack steering north-east, we heard the Bishop's explosive
fog signal fine on the bow and rather too close. Going about we made
another long board to the southward. By next morning we were again
steering northeast, still in poor visibility, when we sighted land close
on the port hand. All agreed that we were east of Land's End and just
about entering Mount's Bay, though to me the presence of some rocky
islets close inshore was puzzling. They must have grown up since the
printing of the chart. A hastily taken sight put us twenty miles to the
west-north-west, somewhere off the north Cornwall coast, the land, if
anywhere, on our starboard hand. Most confusing! Was this the right
continent? As Lecky's editor says: 'Nothing could be more distressing
than running ashore, unless it be a doubt as to which continent that
shore belongs.'

I discarded the sight as being too bad to be true, attributing the
strange result to the poor horizon, the fogged mirror, and Colin's
wrist-watch. I did not even bother to plot the position line that the
sight had given, a line that ran nearly parallel to our course; had that
been done I would have noticed that the line passed close to St Mary's
(which was, of course, the land we had seen) and the Seven Stones
light-vessel. However, we carried on into our supposed Mount's Bay.
It seemed uncommonly wide and although the visibility was poor it

Back at Lymington: Colin Putt, Andrew Harwich, Bob Comlay, Iain Dillon

became every moment more difficult to account for the absence of any land ahead. At length, when we had been sailing for two hours, Bob drew my attention to the Seven Stones lightvessel, just becoming visible less than two miles away on the port beam. The moral seems to be that the most suspect sight is more trustworthy than dead reckoning and guess-work.

By nightfall we were back on the right side of Land's End and the next morning really were in Mount's Bay with Penzance in sight. Outside the bay we hove to, unable to make any ground against an easterly wind that had increased to force 6. The wind did nothing whatever to disperse the fog. We had a close shave in the night with a trawler and early in the morning passed close under the stern of a big Norwegian freighter, hooting away on his foghorn and going dead slow. It was unusual and reassuring to see the Regulations for Preventing Collisions at Sea being so strictly obeyed—perhaps her radar had broken down. The fog lifting and the wind moderating, we paid another visit to Mount's Bay, far enough east this time to see St Michael's Mount instead of Penzance; and in order to let *Sea Breeze* see the place where she had been built seventy-one years ago we went in close to Porthleven.

Since for the last three days the barograph needle had drawn a perfectly straight line across its chart we had little hope of any change in the weather, but the wind did at last veer south and we made a great leap forward to Prawl Point where at night we lay becalmed amidst a stream of shipping. Naturally in these conditions we listened hopefully to the shipping forecast which again gave gale warnings for every area except the Channel where the wind was to be south-west force 5 to 6, and by morning perhaps gale 8. In fact we had a fair wind at south and sailed fast in a perfectly calm sea until with Portland Bill in sight the wind died.

On Sunday the 27th, the last day of the voyage, with a fair wind and the tide under us we went fast past St Alban's Head while Andrew attended to the cooking of a duff to end all duffs to celebrate the event. Like most of our homeward bound duffs it had to be cooked in a bucket to give room and scope enough, and when it appeared on the table, smothered in Golden Syrup, even Colin had to admit that his vision of the higher gluttony had at last materialised. Anchoring for the night off Lymington River we made fast next morning at our old berth, eight days after sighting the Scillies. It had been a frustrating week but at least the sails were dry.

With able and willing hands two days sufficed to strip the rigging and take everything out of the boat and into the store. Colin and Iain lingered in England for a few weeks, returning to the boat at weekends for Colin to lay-up the engine and Iain to repaint the whole of the inside. If they had not had all the climbing they expected, they felt, I think, that our unforeseen and uncalled for adventures in the ice more than made up for that. For my part it had been a good voyage, if not the most successful then certainly the happiest which is almost as important. Those who took part had more or less chosen themselves, so that I could take no credit for that, but only congratulate myself that for once I had sailed with an able and willing crew who thought only of the ship they served and the success of the voyage. With as good a crowd a few years earlier who knows but that something of note might have been accomplished.

Rolling Home, 1970

Bob Comlay

JOHN ANDERSON AND TIM MADGE had an almost impossible task writing their biographies of Tilman. So much of his life was private with only snippets of detail known to a small circle. I have always maintained that his best biography is to be found in his own writing. But there's the rub—his self-deprecating style and masterly gift of understatement simply serve to reinforce the enigma. There are frequent passages which cover dramatic events in such conservative prose that the reader may completely miss the significance of the danger, the hardship or the achievement. There are also few accounts by his companions against which to 'compare and contrast'; Philip Temple's of the 1964 Heard Island expedition is a notable example[*].

The voyage home from Greenland to the Bishop Rock in September 1970 remains the most exhilarating passage I've ever made under sail. I was barely eighteen but that summer left a lasting mark and my memory remains clear. Re-reading the Skipper's account during the preparation of this new edition prompted me to pick up my own diary of the voyage and offer a crew perspective.

We set out from the Danish weather station at Prins Christian Sund on Tuesday September 1st 1970 after spending the summer months working in pack-ice in relatively calm west Greenland waters. The day before, we'd been given a fork-lift truckload of surplus Danish government provisions, and every available locker in *Sea Breeze* was stuffed full, promising culinary delights above and beyond the usual fare of corned beef, pilchards and dried vegetables. The boat, built in 1899 and only a year younger than her owner, was the oldest and most traditionally rigged of Tilman's three Bristol Channel pilot cutters.

---

[*]   *The Sea and the Snow*, fiftieth anniversary edition, Lodestar Books, 2016

Less than forty-eight hours out, my diary records rapidly deterio-rating weather, 'force 9, gusting 10' with '80 strokes of the pump in 10 minutes'. Hove to in these conditions with a heavily reefed main and the staysail backed, we set double watches with the man on deck lashed to the cockpit cleats with the unused jib sheet, while the helmsman just relieved spent two hours on the bilge pump. Sleep was impossible and later that night, exhausted from pumping, I scribbled the first verse of 'Eternal Father, strong to save' in the diary, followed by a rather more optimistic 'I think as long as morale amongst us keeps at its pre-sent level, then *Sea Breeze* will look after us'. While we all shared Colin Putt's view that both boat and Skipper were indestructible, if I'm to be completely honest, that double watch remains the most terrifying four hours I've ever spent at sea.

As daylight broke all hands were fully occupied, with the pair off-watch unpacking the lockers in search of leaks while those on watch carried on pumping and keeping an eye on the gear and the sea. Andrew, the cook and arguably the most important member of the crew, wrestled with his Primus stoves to keep us supplied with tea and soup while directing the unpacking and re-stowing of his stores. Despite the fact that we were hove to at the time, conditions below were cold, wet and far from comfortable. It took us two days to locate the leak, much lower down the hull than we had expected. Once found, it was stemmed by Colin, fitting a strongback across the adjoining frames and pulling the sprung plank back in with a couple of coach screws.

On Tuesday 8th September, one week and six hundred miles out, our third full gale was building. Putting two more rolls in the main, by this point down to about six feet of luff, we noticed the gaff had sprung midway between the peak halliard and the gooseneck. With the wind rising, we lashed the gaff, sail and boom tightly down and rolled on under staysail alone. By this time a significant following sea had built up with a wave height we estimated 'at least 30 feet', and with hundreds of yards between crests. Two or three times a minute we'd be on a crest with an open horizon, before descending to a trough, our visibility down to two or three hundred yards. With the major leak fixed, and faith in the hull restored even if the rig was a disaster area, I vividly recall a glori-ous sunny day under blue skies and bare poles with all warps trailing, at times surfing down the slopes of this big following sea.

The entry for Wednesday 9th notes the failure of the compass light, increasingly important now that the Arctic summer nights were behind us. Thursday 10th records my satisfaction with a successful repair, effected with the aid of a plumber's soldering iron and the Primus stove. The following day the wind moderated enough to enable us to set the topsail as jury main, however, with the sea state still running high, handling the heavy flax canvas sails, getting the gaff down onto the deck for repair, and working out how best to repurpose the topsail took several hours and all available hands.

On Friday 11th Colin succeeded in sawing a pair of splints for the gaff. Shortly afterwards the starboard staysail sheet parted, chafed on the sheave of a block. By Tuesday 15th the gaff was restored and the mainsail set once more. With all sail set, steady motion and good speed, our thoughts clearly turned to improving our lot. An attempt was made to light the Kempsafe oil stove which had steadfastly refused to light since leaving the coast. This time it made amends by rapidly developing into an uncontrolled inferno. Colin, quick to react as always, fired off the ancient dry powder extinguisher which, against all our expectations, actually worked. It had the desired effect on the blaze but did little to improve the condition of the wet sleeping bags and clothing that festooned the saloon in the hope of drying.

That night gale number four blew up causing us to heave to once again. My entry for Friday 18th is brief: 'Fine sunny day, managed to dry clothes and bedding', while Saturday 19th records the Skipper's noon sight putting us seventy miles from the Bishop Rock. The following day, on my watch at 11:00, we picked up the Bishop, right under the bow, exactly as predicted, eighteen days out from Greenland.

In case this remarkable piece of navigation under such trying conditions might be seen as a stroke of luck, I've just checked my diary from the following year's voyage. Once again, the voyage home was dogged by four gales and a sprung gaff, and once again, nineteen days out from Greenland, we sighted the Bishop right on cue. While Tilman's coastal navigation may at times have been called into question, his ocean passage navigation was uncannily accurate.

Bob Comlay
October 2016

H. W. TILMAN

The Collected Edition

For the first time since their original appearance, all fifteen books by H. W. Tilman are being published as single volumes, with all their original photographs, maps and charts. Forewords and afterwords by those who knew him, or who can bring their own experience and knowledge to bear, complement his own understated writing to give us a fuller picture of the man and his achievements. A sixteenth volume is the 1980 biography by J. R. L. Anderson, *High Mountains and Cold Seas*. The books will appear in pairs, one each from his climbing and sailing eras, in order of original publication, at quarterly intervals from September 2015:

Sep 2015	Snow on the Equator
	Mischief in Patagonia
Dec 2015	The Ascent of Nanda Devi
	Mischief Among the Penguins
Mar 2016	When Men & Mountains Meet
	Mischief in Greenland
Jun 2016	Mount Everest 1938
	Mostly Mischief
Sep 2016	Two Mountains and a River
	Mischief Goes South
Dec 2016	China to Chitral
	In Mischief's Wake
Mar 2017	Nepal Himalaya
	Ice With Everything
Jun 2017	Triumph and Tribulation
	High Mountains and Cold Seas

www.tilmanbooks.com